Some of My Best Friends Are

Beauty Queens

Some of My Best Friends Are

Beauty Queens

Life Lessons and Winning Principles
as seen through the reflections of a pageant director

Tricia Woods-Dampier

Some of My Best Friends Are Beauty Queens
Life Lessons and Winning Principles
as seen through the reflections of a pageant director
by Tricia Woods-Dampier

Girl Speak Enterprises
P.O. Box 270072
Littleton, Colorado 80127
tricia@girl-speak.com
www.girl-speak.com

ISBN: 978-0-9830260-0-6

Library of Congress Control Number: 2010915258

Cover and book design: NZ Graphics

Cover photo (from left to right) Emily Stark, Tricia Dampier and Traci Holman
by Image by Roberts

Back cover photo (from left to right) Tiffany Sawyer and Marney Duckworth
by Megan Anderson – Graphique Fine Art Photography

First Edition

Printed in Canada

This book is dedicated to my husband, Russell,
who not only encouraged me to live my dream, but lived it with me.

Preface

In the 2000 movie, *Miss Congeniality* the pageant director, Kathy Morningside, played by Candice Bergen, was portrayed as an uptight, bossy woman wearing a tight fitting "Mary Kay pink" suit obsessed with the world of pageantry. I remembered being momentarily offended by the cartoon characterization before I paused, thought about it for a couple of minutes and realized that there may be a modicum of truth in the portrayal.

I whole-heartedly admit that when I became the Colorado director to the Mrs. America Pageant system, it *was* for all intents and purposes a self-centered endeavor. I wanted to build *my* program to be as prestigious as the Miss Colorado Pageant. I wanted to showcase *my* artistic talents. I wanted to be in control of *my* professional destiny; me—me—me! But in the end the pageant industry provided me with many unique opportunities and one of the most positive was to be able to exalt and encourage *others*.

In part this book is a memoir, as I recount my story of a job that I eventually viewed more as a mission, punctuated by the personal life experiences that shaped my own competitive spirit. It's also part how-to; I do give advice based on the seventeen years I've witnessed the attributes that made a winner and the pitfalls that sometimes defined failure. In any event, even though this book is written primarily through the prism of pageant competition I also think it offers an evaluation of basic life principles on how to live a life that includes taking risks and dealing with challenges.

This book contains the heart-warming and uplifting stories of the women who inspired me to be a good director and maybe even a better person. The stories and lessons contained within these pages were also written for those women who want to expand beyond their comfort zones to realize their full potential, whether that's becoming a pageant titleholder or believing that they can run a marathon, climb a mountain, or campaign for political office.

If for some reason you've picked up this book with the hopes that you'll discover new gown styles—to be told what kind of shoes to wear—or to find a list of statistics on the most winning colors—then this is not the book for you—because, as we all know, style and trends are ever changing. I hope instead that what you *will* find between the pages of this book is the inspiration to dream and the courage to simply try!

Contents

Introduction 13

Chapter One: *Understand The Game You Are Playing* 21

Chapter Two: *Define Your Goals* 33

Chapter Three: *Identify Your Strengths And Weaknesses* 41

Chapter Four: *Faith – The Power Of Believing That You Can* 49

Chapter Five: *Be Fearless – Not Reckless* 59

Chapter Six: *Be The Original God Created You To Be* 71

Chapter Seven: *Choose To Inspire Those Around You* 81

Chapter Eight: *Learn From Your Experience* 91

Chapter Nine: *Enjoy The Journey* 103

Chapter Ten: *Dreaming Is Easy – Dreams Are Not* 113

Chapter Eleven: *Commit To Prepare – Prepare To Win* 127

Chapter Twelve: *Blessings Beyond The Crown* 155

Acknowledgments 177

About the Author 179

Janet Horvath – Mrs. Colorado 1992

Introduction

"Dreams are the touchstones of our character."
~ Henry David Thoreau – American Author

On the day that I packed up my royal blue Datsun B-210 in the fall of 1975 and headed out for Colorado State University, had someone asked me to make a list of possible career paths I doubt "pageant director" would have made the top one hundred choices. But life has a way of taking on a rhythm of its own, and in 1992 I did just that, I became the Colorado director to the Mrs. America Pageant system.

It's not that I had anything against people who produce pageant competitions or even pageant contestants, but at *that* point in my life even though I knew who Miss America was I had never actually seen a pageant. Probably because like most middle class homes in the '60s and '70s the evenings belonged to my father and he was in control of the one and only, black and white television set. Tuning into the Miss America Pageant wouldn't have been his first choice for decompressing after a long day at work or in lieu of watching weekend football.

It wasn't until the mid-'80s that I met my first "pageant girl" while dancing with Pure Gold, the cheerleaders for the USFL Denver Gold football team. Actually there were two former Miss Colorado USA title-holders on the squad, along with my friend Liz who had just recently been crowned Miss Littleton. She spent a lot of time that year preparing for the state competition and I became one of her biggest fans. By pure osmosis I became fascinated with the process.

I consider myself to be competitive by nature, but in the era in which I grew up, young women weren't encouraged to compete in sports. Didn't matter anyway, I broke two fingers in high school gym class, one playing basketball and the other playing volleyball, before the teacher pulled me out and put me in a conditioning class instead (a '70s version of an aerobics class, minus the *pump-you-up* music). I did, however, enjoy competing in music and cheerleading for most of my school days.

I queried my friends on how they became involved in pageant competition and decided to enter my five-year-old niece, Ara, in a local Miss Cinderella competition held in center court at the Westminster Mall. I assumed that it was too late for me, since by then I was already married. My friend Liz casually mentioned the Mrs. America Pageant and encouraged me to enter; the seed was planted, my competitive nature kicked in, and well, simply put, there was no turning back.

With no experience and little information to go on, I first competed for the title of Mrs. Colorado in 1987 and placed first runner-up. In hindsight I attribute my success to a bit of beginner's luck. I was the fresh-faced rookie who had lots of spirit, a great dress (I learned that much from watching my friend Liz), a peppy almost choppy walk and a cavalier attitude about the competition. In short, I was likable and I had the unwavering belief that I *could* win. In fact it never crossed my mind that I couldn't!

Not to be discouraged I re-entered as fast as I could after the 1987 competition. To this day I like to joke that if there had been a sign-up sheet on stage that night I would have been the first to enter. My preparations included watching all of the televised national pageants, attending every state competition, and I began judging little local competitions. (My resume with dance and music qualified me in many small circles.) I took copious notes, bought yet another gown, had professional photos taken, and engaged a coach to teach me how to walk the "pageant walk" more elegant and a little less peppy. After the preliminary round of competition my family (God bless them they are the most honest people on earth) wanted to know *what the heck* I was doing. What happened to Tricia? Who was that "robotron" gliding across the stage? I had mastered all of the pageant skills, but in turn I'd left my most valuable asset at home—my individuality. I had officially turned into a boring, cookie-cutter competitor.

Well as it turned out, once again I placed first runner-up! I was heartbroken and for a couple of weeks considered giving up. I quickly got over it and decided to apply the lessons I'd learned and give it another shot. Not to say that I didn't shed some tears in the following forty-eight hours, but I wasn't willing to be defeated by my defeat! I must admit that my family was pretty skeptical at this point. They weren't sure if they should encourage me to continue or not. In the end the decision was mine and I'm truly grateful that my husband, parents and sister didn't try to talk me out of competing yet one more time.

I was also grateful that during my younger years I competed in band and cheerleading and had actually failed miserably upon several occasions. That failure fueled a can-do attitude that's not only served me well in competition, but also during the ups and downs of life. I'm not a pro-ponent of the "self-esteem movement" that entitles every child who competes to be a winner. The fact is, sometimes you win and sometimes you don't. There's absolutely no shame in failing—failing taught me to be gracious in loss and fostered the attitude that with the right amount of work and perseverance I would eventually succeed.

I did indeed enter the 1989 Mrs. Colorado Pageant competition. Waiting another year to try again seemed like an eternity. I can't imagine what it must be like for Olympic athletes who have to wait four long years before they can "Go for the Gold" one more time. I continued working on my walk, I enrolled myself in a speech and debate class at the local community college to sharpen my speaking skills, bought a different dress, (which really wasn't necessary) and taught dance classes at night to pay for it. But this time Tricia showed up to compete, not a cheap imitation of someone else, and it turned out to be the winning formula. On April 29, one day before my twelfth wedding anniversary,

I was crowned Mrs. Colorado 1989—a joyful event no doubt, but an event that I had no idea would ultimately change the course of my life.

So how exactly does one become a pageant director? For me, I do believe it was "Divine Providence." Five years earlier I was working in the family finance business, making a more than decent salary, with predictable hours, wonderful benefits and the promise of a secure future. There was only one problem—I wasn't good at it, and in turn it made my forty-hour work week very arduous. One day as I sat at my typewriter, tears involuntarily trickled down my face. I stood up, walked into my father's office and I quit! His kindness made leaving easy, plus he might have actually been a little relieved given I had no real talent for the business. Both of my parents were always big on teaching my sister and me the importance of doing what you like and then doing it to the best of your ability.

In the years that followed, I worked as an aerobics instructor, I taught beginning dance to adult students at a popular dance studio, and modeled for a local talent agency. I worked enough to contribute to the household income, but still hadn't found the right career fit when in December of 1991 I got a phone call from the vice president of the Mrs. America Pageant asking me if I would be interested in applying for the Colorado directorship. I jumped at the opportunity and by the end of January 1992 an agreement had been reached. My contract required me to wrap up the '92 pageant season by the middle of June giving me only four and a half months to produce my first competition; *no problem*, or so I thought.

In a short period of time I needed to set up a corporation and have business cards and letterhead printed. I had to book a venue, recruit contestants, recruit sponsors for a prize package and write a script. I had to find a celebrity emcee, five qualified judges, a certified public accountant to audit the pageant and a vocalist to fill in the entertainment segments. I had to make music selections, design a set and come up with some creative choreography. The cliché "ignorance is bliss" surely applied, but

Chapter One

Understand The Game You Are Playing

"If you're going to play the game properly, you'd better know every rule."

~ Barbara Jordan – African-American, Texas Congresswoman 1973-1979

During my tenure as the Colorado state director many people had asked me the question, "Why do women compete in pageants?" I can honestly say that I never really understood the question. At first I attempted to explain pageant competition, but I could tell that the definitional answer didn't sufficiently satisfy their curiosity. And then one day it hit me. The next time I was asked, "Why do women compete in pageants?" I replied, "The same reason people climb mountains—because they can!" The answer would almost always evoke a puzzled look and then a slight sign of acknowledgment, followed by a hesitant, but accepting nod of the head. To me it was the perfect answer. Why does anyone compete? Because competition feeds the human soul; it nurtures our ambition and fuels the drive and desire to better ourselves. Competition animates our sometimes rather mundane lives; it inspires a fundamental need to be our best and strive to be the best that God created us to be.

Pageantry is not unlike any other sport or competition. In order to best prepare yourself you first need to have a basic understanding of the rules. I offered each Mrs. Colorado contestant a complimentary one hour consultation with me to discuss her pageant preparations. As a contestant once myself, I remembered how frustrating it was to obtain information on how to begin. Colorado isn't a big pageant state like the southern states or some of the more cosmopolitan states like California and New York, so our resources for information, wardrobe and coaches used to be very limited. It has since changed.

Besides giving the contestants a chance to get their "road map" to competition, meeting with them also gave me an opportunity to get to know them on a personal basis. While the process was incredibly time consuming, giving over fifty women a one hour appointment, it turned out to be an unexpected blessing. They were no longer just a number or a city representative, but real women with real dreams, many of whom had faced formidable challenges and led wildly interesting lives.

For some reason, most of the "Mrs." contestants were first time pageant competitors. I eventually came to the conclusion that competing in a pageant is something that many little girls dream about at some time during the course of their lifetimes. If they had the opportunity to do it as young women then it was no longer on their "fantasy wish list." The Mrs. America Pageant system offered a second chance to women who had married young or married women who had aged out of the Miss competitions.

My goal in the one-on-one preparation session was to make sure the state finalists had all the information that they needed to proceed with their choices on how to prepare. I wanted to make sure they *understood the game that they were playing.* Over time I had fine-tuned my skills on how to disseminate that information in a way that made sense to the average woman.

I would generally give them the run down on the specifics of the three categories of competition: personal interview, physical fitness, and evening gown. I would also describe to them the way in which they would be scored in each segment. I believe you should understand the pageant's scoring system and the basic profile of the people who will be selected as judges. Who would blindly sign up for any sport or contest and not know the rules? The answer is nobody who had any aspirations of winning.

We first discussed the importance of the personal interview, how to dress, the format, a one-on-one interview vs. a judging panel, appropriate make-up and hair style, the four minute time frame and what kind of questions they could expect to be asked. You will want to know if the interview will be taken off of a submitted biography form and if political and religious questions can be asked. You may also be required to have a platform and address current events. In most pageants the interview is usually the first preliminary round of competition. In my opinion it's without a doubt the most important phase as well. Besides being your "first impression" it's also one of the few opportunities you'll have to reveal your intelligence, humor and communication style.

Simply put, if you split pageant competition into two categories, one being substance and one being style, the personal interview is the bulk of your substance score. I've seen really beautiful women miss making the first cut because they gave a horrible personal interview and the judges never bothered to look at them again.

It helps, if in advance, you do a little homework on the competition you are about to enter. What does the pageant stand for? What are they looking for in a titleholder? In the case of the Mrs. America Pageant system, it defines the optimum Mrs. America delegate as the contemporary married woman; a beautiful yet approachable woman who can represent the ideals of family and marriage. Other various pageant systems are searching for spokesmodels to promote their brand, some are looking for a young woman who can make a social or political statement, and some are just looking for a "glamorous icon."

As a state director, I didn't feel that it was necessary for *my* contestants to be prepared to answer questions on hot button topics like abortion, gun control and illegal immigration. I wasn't looking for the next president of the United States. I was looking for an ambassador to represent my program. However, there are some pageant systems that will require you to have opinions on such issues, so ask the competition organizers in advance what will be expected of you and prepare accordingly.

Most pageants have some type of a swimsuit/physical fitness competition. While it has, in recent history, been a point of social contention for mainstream society, I've never had a problem with it. When did it become politically incorrect to be proud of physical fitness? Consider this; every day Americans seem to have no problem with the following:

- Watching scantily clad women play beach volleyball in the Olympics.
- We tolerate, if not endure, the sight of women wearing a thong bikini on the family beach in Waikiki.
- We watch televised "award shows" to check out cultural celebrities like Britney Spears and Jennifer Lopez wearing nothing more than a hanky for a dress.
- Someone in the P.R. Department at Victoria's Secret thought it was a clever idea to dress up gorgeous women in wings and underwear and call it a "Christmas Special."
- Oh, and where's the social outrage over the swimsuit edition of *Sports Illustrated*? I don't get it—isn't *Sports Illustrated* a publication devoted to sports coverage not swimsuit fashion? It's perfectly acceptable for women to wear see-through bikinis in a magazine dedicated to sports, but somehow competing in a pageant wearing sexy/modest swimwear is objectifying women? I think not!

Excuse my fifteen seconds of righteous indignation, but the moral platitude that somehow swimsuit competition marginalizes women reeks of hypocrisy. It's been my experience that many seriously overweight women decided to enter the pageant as a way to motivate them to lose weight and become healthier. Unlike the modeling profession that requires women to be "stick skinny," pageant competition encourages a toned, physically fit appearance.

Then there's the evening gown competition. Honestly I've seen everything from women who tried to rework their wedding dresses to wearing an old prom dress and let me be the first one to tell you, that on so many levels, this is just not going to work! I often times used a hypothetical sports analogy to explain why choosing the proper wardrobe was crucial in this kind of competition since so many Americans can easily relate to sports.

There was a talented man who decided to try out for the Denver Broncos football team as a walk-on competitor. He was young, tall, strong, muscular and fast. Everyone who saw him thought it was a given that he would make the first cut; but on the day of tryouts he showed up to compete wearing hockey gear.

Okay, this is where I would inevitably get a blank stare like, "You've got to be kidding me?" But the point of the story was that while he possessed all of the physical God-given talents to play the game of football, he really didn't have a fundamental understanding of the position he was competing for.

Likewise, I was always perplexed by women who would balk at the idea of wearing make-up. The most common excuse I'd get was, "I don't like wearing make-up; it's just not me." For these women I found another analogy effective in trying to convince them of the need to "play the game."

I'd begin by asking them if they enjoyed going to the theater and we might even discuss a favorite play or musical. I'd ask them if they had perhaps had the chance to see the *Phantom of the Opera*, one of my personal favorites. And most women had seen it or at the very least were familiar with the famous image of the main character. I would then ask, "How would you feel if you went to see the *Phantom* on Broadway and the performances were moving and the sets were phenomenal, but on *that* particular night the actor playing the lead role decided not to wear his mask and make-up?"

Begrudgingly, the contestant acknowledged that they *would* feel disappointed. Make no mistake about it, pageant competition is about glamour. The reason people are attracted to watching the telecasts is the same reason why they tune in to watch the red carpet event at the Oscars. It's all about the "image." We want to see the beautiful celebrities, in their designer gowns with their glamorous make-up and hair-dos. Pageantry is no different.

The biggest myth plaguing pageant competition today is that it's a "pretty" contest, which strongly suggests that there's no skill whatsoever involved in winning. From an outsider's perspective I completely understand the misperception. Let's face it, the term "beauty queen" has perpetuated the idea that the crowned winner won because of her beauty. And while I lovingly used the phrase in the title of this book as a term of endearment; the verbiage within the industry is largely considered antiquated. The politically correct term is now "titleholder."

Secondly, the public at large only sees the end result. The televised final competition showcases beautiful women, with rockin' bodies, who walk the catwalk in glamorous gowns, make-up, jewelry and hair styles; who at the most only have to answer one question to show off her intellectual prowess. People should only know how much dedication and hard work goes into competing. To some degree I fault the upper management of pageantry for doing a poor job of keeping up with the times and failing to market the competitors as real people who tenaciously work to make it to their respective "Super Bowls."

Years ago in an attempt to attract a larger female audience, sports programming began running personal life stories about athletes. Their stories inspired a desire to root for them and to root for the team; viewers now had a personal investment in seeing them succeed. All of a sudden their athletic abilities didn't seem so effortless. Wouldn't it be nice if every televised pageant profiled a handful of contestants, whose stories would only be seen by the viewing audience and not the judge's panel? That way the average person as well as pageant devotees would feel as though they got a glimpse into the life of a real person, a real competitor.

Recently one of my all-time favorite Miss Americas, Gretchen Carlson, Miss America 1989, and now a morning anchor on Fox & Friends, sat down for a one-on-one interview with Rush Limbaugh who was invited to be a celebrity judge at the 2010 Miss America Pageant. Early in the exchange he admitted to being surprised at the caliber of competitors. I couldn't help myself—I shouted halleluiah—finally a credible social figure was acknowledging the serious side to pageant competition.

Here is a transcribed portion of the interview:

Carlson:

…And now here we are in Las Vegas and you're one of the judges of the Miss America Pageant. What made you decide to say yes to their request?

Limbaugh:

Well, I've always been intrigued with this. I'm like everybody else, I grew up watching it. So I decided to do it and only then did I find out what the real work commitment is. I mean it is—folks—this is a big time serious thing. One thing, there is nothing frivolous about this. There's no frivolity at all. It's very serious. And these women have devoted their lives, in most cases, to this week…

Carlson:

Have you been more impressed or less impressed with the quality and caliber of the women that you've met?

Limbaugh:

There's a group of fifty-three here. And I would say that the vast majority of them are confident and poised as they speak. That's one of the things I was looking for. We interview each one of them for about ten minutes and that's about fourteen hours over two days. And there's nowhere for them to hide.

Carlson:

Especially from you.

Limbaugh:

Gretchen, I've talked to women here who know more about various political issues than elected people I've talked to on the phone.

It was almost comical how animated Mr. Limbaugh got when trying to convince people of the fact that the competition and the women involved were not "frivolous." Those of us who have seen and or lived the competition from the inside out already knew that.

A week earlier on a Sunday morning televised church service a prominent theologian, Dr. Robert H. Schuller interviewed, Miss California, Kristy Cavinder. During the interview he asked the question, "So is there any work in trying to become Miss California or Miss America?"

Now I don't believe for one minute that Dr. Schuller didn't think there was work involved, instead I think he asked the question to dispel the myth that it's a contest for "pretty girls" who just "poof" magically show up, perfectly coifed, to parade in front of the cameras.

She answered, "It was a lot of work. I spent six months (the six months between being crowned Miss California and going to the Miss America Pageant) working on interview preparation, preparing for my talent and the swimsuit competition. It's a lot of work, but through the process of the training and the gym workouts and all of the mock interviews that I did, I really learned who I was as a person and I became more confident in who I was and what I believed in."

If you only glean one thing from this chapter; know that if you enter a pageant you are entering a serious competition that will indeed require a skill set, mental strength, a determined attitude, and a can-do spirit. Or in plain English, "pretty slackers" need not apply.

Understand The Game You Are Playing

The Take Away

- Research the competition you are considering entering.
- Don't be afraid to ask the organizers questions relating to the scoring system and the framework of the judging panel.
- Prepare a healthy comprehensive diet and exercise regimen to be competitive in swimsuit competition.
- Make sure your wardrobe selections and make-up are in keeping with the competition you wish to win.

Gina DelVecchio – Mrs. Colorado 1998

Chapter Two

Define Your Goals

*"Our goals can only be reached through a vehicle
of a plan, in which we must fervently believe,
and upon which we must vigorously act.
There is no other route to success."*

~ Stephen A. Brennan – Basketball Coach

When meeting with new contestants, I loved to pose the question,
"When the pageant is over, what three things do you wish to have
achieved from participating in this competition?"

It was usually the first thing I asked after we had exchanged some
pleasantries and small talk. A majority of the women actually had a hard
time answering the question. So, before you read on, stop and take a
minute to write down the three things you hope to gain from competing
in the competition you are considering.

The best answer I'd ever heard to that question was given by a woman
named Beverly Truscheit. Without hesitation and with a laugh in her
delivery she answered, "The Crown, The Crown, The Crown, is there
anything else?" I couldn't help but smile. I congratulated her on knowing *exactly* what she wanted. Unfortunately and most surprisingly, many
women didn't include winning as one of their top three goals. Once they

33

had verbally fumbled around trying to come up with three things they hoped to achieve I would ask them, "Well, do you want to win?"

After I got the confused double-take look they would almost always reply, "Of course I want to win!"

To which I responded, "Then why didn't you say you wanted to win?"

They would come up with reasons like I didn't want to sound presumptuous or the classic "nice" answer: I didn't want to seem boastful. I venture to guess that if you were to ask a man if he wanted or thought he could win the golf tournament, city softball championship or the winter bowling league, he wouldn't hesitate to respond with a resounding, "Heck yes I can win!" Coming up with the "nice" answer probably wouldn't have even occurred to him.

There's a real difference between arrogance and pride, as well, there is a real difference between timidity and humility. In a message titled: *The Five Basics of Hope Filled Faith,* Dr. Robert H. Schuller the founder of the famous Crystal Cathedral Church explained that humility and healthy pride are different sides of the same coin, like heads and tails. The conclusion drawn from the analogy is that the coin has equal value whether you've got heads or tails up.

The humble person is grateful for his or her gifts and achievements. Their success is transferable. On the other hand, egotism or arrogance is a narcissistic view of one's accomplishments. It benefits nobody.

Humility and pride in effect complement one another. It's *okay* to be competitive and to want to win. In fact if you can't define winning as one of your main objectives, the truth of the matter is, it probably won't happen. Defining our goals and committing them to paper is a powerful tool when competing. You've got to want to make it happen for winning to become a reality. Mind you, I said, *make* it happen not *wish* it to happen. I liked challenging my contestants to select three goals, forcing them to evaluate their true intentions as well as how to achieve success. If we are mindful of what we want and have been encouraged to define how to reach those goals, the chances are, they are more likely to come to fruition.

And ultimately most women were actually invigorated by the exercise as it challenged them to declare how they intended to make themselves competitive. The reason I asked for three things was because I wanted the contestants to think through the experience and consciously participate with specific objectives in mind.

In 1996 I had a contestant who told me, "I've just moved to Colorado from Mississippi and I joined the pageant in hopes of making new connections." She didn't win that year, but she did make friends and when she returned to the pageant in 1998, Gina DelVecchio took home the Mrs. Colorado title and crown. But if you were to ask her today what was the one *most* valuable thing she gained from competing in the pageant, her answer would be that she met a couple of women whom to this day she still considers her "best friends." Being *mindful* that she wanted to make friends prompted her to reach out and seek those relationships.

More than a few women joined the pageant in hopes of motivating themselves to lose their college-cafeteria thighs, their baby weight or their middle-age spread. Once they had listed that as a goal, I encouraged them to follow up with a small list of ideas on how to achieve weight loss. This exercise focuses the competitor on identifying the goal and then designing a strategy to make it happen. Again, I'm a big proponent of identifying not only the goals, but the plan on how to actually turn desire into action. My question would be, "How much weight do you want to lose?"

I always found it completely ridiculous when someone would say, "I don't know," or "I don't really want to put a number on it." I would almost always kindly suggest to them that if you don't know how much you want to lose then how will you know when you've accomplished your goal? I think before our meetings were over they had seen the light. Again, you can go through life wishing to lose weight, but unless you have a plan of action, in fact, all you are really doing is wishing.

Aside from, "The Crown, The Crown, The Crown," the answer I liked the most was when women identified that they wanted to compete to increase their self-confidence. I do believe that competing in just about any activity increases confidence because the very first step in competing is believing that you can.

Kimberlee Jo Stiles was a woman who had admittedly struggled with weight and self-confidence for much of her life. She entered my pageant in 1996. I personally found her interesting, but a little aloof. During pageant weekend, she participated in all of the activities, but remained quiet and reserved. I wasn't sure if she was actually enjoying herself, and then on top of it she didn't place. That's usually a "deal breaker" for those people who are uncomfortable with the process.

When I was ready to accept applications for the following year, Kim called my office and requested entry information. I remembered being surprised that she wanted to enter again given I wasn't entirely sure she'd had a positive experience.

As it turns out, I was mistaken. To me she had appeared distant, when in fact she was quietly observing every moment of her competition experience. She told me in that conversation, "Tricia, just before I left the dressing room for evening gown competition I turned around to look in the mirror and for the first time in a long time, I saw a beautiful woman looking back!"

Once we "grow up" and leave the learning environment that school provides, most of us fall into the routine of our everyday lives. We're now responsible for a mortgage, a car payment, living expenses, a spouse, maybe children and very little time is left to continue developing our personal skills. Competing often challenges us to devote some time to reflect on who we are and who we want to be. In some strange way it gives us permission to be a little self-focused and maybe even forces us to set aside time to take personal inventory of our lives.

And, indeed, I witnessed the increase of self-image in *most* of the women I worked with. Setting goals and actually accomplishing them can be a very powerful thing!

Define Your Goals

The Take Away:

- Give yourself permission to want to win.
- Write out a list of goals.
- Design a plan on how to achieve those goals.
- Seek out the proper resources to help you attain your aspirations.

Elisabeth Cartmill – Mrs. Colorado 2003

Chapter Three

Identify Your Strengths And Weaknesses

"If you don't know where you are going, you'll end up someplace else."
~ Yogi Berra – Major League Baseball Coach

Over the years, my job evolved from essentially being an "event organizer" to a position that called me to mentor women. As the director of the pageant, I encouraged contestants to define their strengths and weaknesses since that's the only way to fully understand where one wants to go and actually make a plan on how to get there. For some reason many women I worked with struggled with both concepts. They were reluctant to identify their strengths and many wanted to ignore any shortcomings they may have viewed as roadblocks to success.

Sometime in the fall of 2005 I received a phone call from a woman who was expressing interest in competing. Not an unusual day by any means as I did a lot of marketing and advertising after children returned to school from summer vacation. The call started with the standard conversation about the pageant, but quickly turned to something different when the woman on the other end of the phone asked me if the "walk" was a major factor in judging pageant competition. Years earlier she had broken her back and as a result now walked with a limp.

I paused for a moment searching for the "right" answer. After all, pageantry is like any other sport or competition; you need participants in order for the event to be relevant. I didn't want to lose a potential competitor by saying, "Yes the modeling is important." But I had to tell the truth. I took a deep breath and after a thoughtful exhale I honestly replied, "Yes, the walk is very important." But I continued, "Now that you've identified that as a possible weakness, let's discuss a strategy to overcome it."

Carrie Basse was an eighteen-year-old college freshman who on one fateful evening had volunteered to be the designated driver for her roommates and friends. Returning home late in the evening they soon discovered that they were locked out of their apartment. Since she had been deemed the "responsible party" Carrie scaled the roof to break into a second story window. She slipped, fell and broke her back. The immediate diagnosis was an L-one compression fracture leaving chips of shattered vertebra lodged in her spinal cord. The prognosis was a fifty/fifty chance of ever walking again. In an emergency surgery doctors removed a rib and fused it with cadaver bone; then fused her spine with a metal plate and screws.

Seven days later she left the hospital in a wheelchair. Soon thereafter she embarked on a regimen of physical therapy for three hours a day, four days a week and would eventually walk again with the assistance of a walker. Therapists predicted that she would never bear children, hike, bike, or run and would never again wear high heels. Now it's important to remember this last detail as it will play a small role in her decision to enter the pageant.

Eventually she graduated from the walker to using two canes, then one cane and over a period of years she would in fact walk again without the assistance of any apparatus. In 1994 she made a brave decision to leave her family and the familiarity of friends and community behind to move to Colorado in search of a new beginning. It was in Colorado that she met her future husband, who embraced her disability and encouraged her to dismiss the skeptics.

After marrying Michael, she was diagnosed with adhesive arachnoiditis, which is common in people who have suffered a back injury. Adhesive arachnoiditis is a debilitating, degenerative disease characterized by severe stinging and burning pain and neurological problems caused by an inflammation of the arachnoid lining, which is one of the three linings that surround the brain and spinal cord. The inflammation causes constant irritation, scarring and binding of nervous roots and blood vessels.

When I interviewed Carrie while writing this book, I asked her why she had decided to enter a pageant in the face of all that she had to overcome. She told me it was part of a greater plan to battle the depression she suffered after being diagnosed with adhesive arachnoiditis. She had adopted a daughter, back-packed the Grand Canyon and now she wanted, once again, to walk in high heels; defying the earlier predictions of her physical therapists.

Surely, Carrie Basse faced serious challenges entering a pageant competition where the *walk* was significant in defining oneself as poised and physically self-confident on stage. In that very first conversation, I informed her that if she capitalized on her strengths, which we would end up defining in a subsequent meeting and worked to shore up her obvious weakness, I believed that she would prove to be competitive.

Part of our game plan included walking lessons from one of the top modeling coaches in Colorado and aside from that I later found out that Carrie had solicited instruction from her daughter's ballet teacher to help her with balance and coordination.

There were fifty state finalists competing for the crown in 2006. Needless to say that the shear numbers would inevitably make this event competitive. I had always co-emceed my production along with a local media personality and unlike many other directors, I chose not to know which contestants had made the first cut until the certified public accountant actually handed us the envelope on stage seconds before the big announcement. That night as we began reading the names of the semi-finalists, there it was, there was *her* name, contestant number fifteen, Carrie Basse. My heart momentarily jumped with excitement for her.

The top fifteen semifinalists were then required to re-compete in swimsuit competition. Now this, of course, would prove to be Carrie's biggest challenge since it is much harder to disguise your walk in a swimsuit, compared to an evening gown. The field would be narrowed from fifteen to ten based on this one category. If you would have asked me, I probably would have predicted that this might be the end of the road for Carrie. However, when I opened the envelope to announce the top ten, there was her name again, contestant number fifteen, Carrie Basse; what a stunning personal victory.

That night when the pageant was over I remained on stage as I always did to meet and greet audience members, give hugs to contestants, oversee the publicity photos and work with the stage crew. I saw Carrie making her way through the crowd approaching me with tears streaming down her face. Finally reaching me she proclaimed, "I will *never* enter this pageant again!" I was taken aback not expecting this kind of reaction. She continued, "Because I've accomplished what I thought I *couldn't* do!" I let out a sigh of relief; as a pageant director you never really know how disappointment will manifest itself in contestants by the end of the weekend.

Later in a telephone conversation, I asked Carrie to sum up her overall experience and this is what she said:

"Since the pageant, my insecurities about the way I walk no longer matter. If I could do it in front of two thousand people, I no longer worry about what the people in the grocery store think of me."
~ Carrie Basse – Mrs. Elbert County 2006

Her story could have fit into several chapters of this book, but I thought it best illuminated the concept that if you decide to enter *any* competition, first identify your strengths and weaknesses, and then challenge yourself to capitalize on your positives and figure out a way to minimize your negatives.

Identify Your Strengths and Weaknesses

The Take Away

- Acknowledge that you have both strengths and weaknesses.
- Make a list of your abilities.
- Make a list of the things that might pose a challenge to you.
- Be okay with not being "perfect," instead strive toward progress.
- Outline a plan to tackle your identified weaknesses.

Christina Sacha – Mrs. Colorado 2008

Chapter Four

Faith — The Power Of Believing That You Can

"Now faith is the substance of things hoped for, the evidence of things not seen."
~ Hebrews 11:1 – Holy Bible King James Version

E very year I was amazed at the women who would call me and ask questions like: Do *short* women win? Can *tall* women win? Do women *without* children win? Can women *with* big families win? Do women *over* thirty win? Can women *under* thirty win? I struggled to understand the reasoning behind these questions until one day I had what Oprah calls an "Aha Moment." These women were already making a list of reasons why they *couldn't* win. Unlike identifying your strengths and weaknesses, these women had already determined that they couldn't win based on imaginary drawbacks. It was as if before they began they were already trying to convince themselves that they couldn't succeed; they were making a list of perceived shortcomings and were already writing a personal narrative for failure.

While I would spend a considerable amount of time answering their questions, I soon figured out that even though these women possessed a seed of hope that they *could* compete (or they wouldn't have bothered to call me in the first place), they didn't really believe that they *could* be competitive. Most often, no matter how much time I spent with them or how many fears I had laid to rest, they couldn't bring themselves to enter the pageant. I felt sorry for these women because the lack of faith in one-self can be the most debilitating condition in life.

So how *do* you develop the faith to believe in yourself? I would imagine that many sports psychologists have built their careers working with competitors who needed to answer that question. I think that the courage to believe in yourself can be developed over the course of a life-time, if you don't come by it naturally, but you have to really want it.

I learned the art of competition through activities like music and cheerleading; popular past-times for females during the '60s and '70s. I began my music career in the third grade playing the clarinet in the band at Tomasita Elementary. During that era, music education was taught in early childhood development, as opposed to waiting until middle school like it's done now. I'm a lucky beneficiary of that philosophy and public school program.

The story begins when the director of the band, Mr. Chavez, came into our classroom and played the clarinet. He then asked those of us who were interested in joining the band to go home and persuade our parents to buy us an instrument. I still laugh at myself because had he walked into the classroom playing a tuba, this underweight, little third-grader would have gone home and asked her dad and mom to buy her a tuba. Mr. Chavez's infectious enthusiasm was responsible for instilling in me a deep love of music that would last a lifetime.

My parents found a way to get me a clarinet on a lease/purchase agreement. After telling me that they weren't sure they could afford to buy me one, a couple of days later without much fanfare they surprised me with a brand-new clarinet displayed upon my bed. To this day it stands out as one of the most precious moments of my life; and thus began the days of learning to nurture my competitive spirit.

Okay, so now you know I'm a self-proclaimed "band geek," but the intellectual glory of being a member of the band was that your position depended on how competitive you wanted to be. There were four categories for each instrument section; in my case first clarinet, second clarinet, third clarinet and fourth clarinet, and there were usually four to five students in each section. Your standing depended upon your ability and willingness to compete for the position.

Musically speaking I think I was probably naturally gifted; however, my nerves always caused me a great deal of angst. Music came easy to me, but when I was being challenged for my position or when I decided to challenge someone for a new position, I was an internal mess. And unfortunately for me that anxiety began at an early age; by the seventh grade I was experiencing severe physical and emotional distress relating to competition. I confided in my mother how important it was for me to hold a position in the first clarinet section as it provided me with the best opportunities to play choice parts in the band performances and by then it was a matter of personal pride.

She shared a scripture with me that I wrote on the cover of my music book. Of all my childhood memorabilia, like my cheerleading megaphone, pom-poms and dried up homecoming corsages, all of which eventually hit the trashcan, I saved that particular beginner's music book and I'm glad I did. The Bible verse that appears on the cover is Philippians 4:13: "For I can do all things through Christ who strengthens me."

At the very core of my self-confidence was the belief in something bigger than me and even when I was flooded with toxic self-doubt, I knew that I could pray for a calm spirit. My mother didn't teach me to pray for things that I *hadn't* earned, but rather to pray that God would give me a spirit of confidence that would allow me to perform at my optimum level.

My father's job required many moves, and as a shy, even awkward child, I always found it hard to re-establish myself in new schools. The summer before my eighth grade year my father's job had relocated us once again, this time from Oklahoma, where the school I attended was huge, to Colorado where my family moved to a much smaller community, and of course a much smaller school.

Auditioning for a position in this band should have been a no-brainer, but at the end of the auditioning process I was dead last. I went from playing in the first clarinet section of a big school to one chair away from being in the secondary, remedial band in a really small school. *Last* chair in the *last* fourth clarinet section! I couldn't have been more devastated, but most of all I was angry at myself. I knew I was better than that. I failed only because I lacked the mental discipline and confidence in my abilities. Even though I can make light of it some forty-odd years later it was a humiliating and painful experience. Now, I wasn't just the "new kid," *oh no*, now, I was the "dumb new kid!"

I'm actually grateful that I experienced crushing defeat early in competition. For one thing I think it's easier to bounce back from disappointment when you're young, and in hindsight it was the losses that nurtured my can-do attitude, not the wins.

Looking back, I'm proud of that skinny, new kid, band geek because I wasn't going to be warming that last chair in the fourth clarinet section for very long. I knew I was better than my performance, but I was pretty sure that I needed a couple of private lessons to regain my self-confidence. When it came time to challenge a student for his or her position I had no intention of eking my way up the chain, I went right for Scott Linkenfelter's first chair, in the first section. I wound up second chair in the first clarinet section, but Scott Linkenfelter's position still wasn't safe. I continued my private lessons, practiced an hour every night and by the end of my eighth grade year I had beat him out for the top spot. I had redeemed myself and the belief in my ability to compete was completely restored along with a little self-respect.

As a pageant director I often silently wondered how many people would have eventually won the crown had they just continued to believe that they could win. I have a hunch that there were quite a few.

In 2004, a beautiful, blonde named Christina Sacha entered the Mrs. Colorado Pageant competition. She had spent a lifetime in pageantry and won many local and state titles as well as a national and international title. Let's just say that she didn't lack for experience or self-confidence. Having come from a much larger state, she later confessed that she may have underestimated the level of competition in Colorado. That year she placed in the top ten.

She returned to the pageant in 2006 after the birth of her second child, but this time was prepared for the caliber of competition. She placed first runner-up, but that night I witnessed a real winner on stage when she joyfully celebrated Marney Duckworth as the new Mrs. Colorado. Christina definitely raised the bar on good sportsmanship!

In 2007 she came back, needless to say with the same determined attitude, a nearly flawless performance and the same gracious spirit, but disappointingly, once again, placed first runner-up. By now the Mrs. Colorado staff, volunteers and emcee had deemed her the *best* first runner-up we had ever seen. She applauded the winner, smiled in all the publicity photos and remained on stage afterwards to greet her supporters. You see a real winner is just as gracious in loss as he or she is in victory.

In the wings of the stage that night her husband asked how she was feeling. She replied with a deep sigh, "I feel like I just dropped the winning touchdown pass in the Super Bowl for the second time. I think I'm done!"

If you read my introduction you know that I was probably the only person on stage that night who could completely relate to the position of being first runner-up two years in a row. For some reason coming that close and not realizing your goal can challenge the *faith* in believing that you can.

I gently consoled her not really knowing if I had the stomach to encourage her to try again. By this time in my career I was keenly aware of my contestants' feelings and I wasn't sure that I should try to persuade someone so vulnerable to return when there was no real guarantee of a different outcome. I knew that decision had to be hers.

When writing this chapter I asked Christina a couple of questions to solidify what I thought I understood to be her experience. I first asked her, "Did you ever doubt that you could win?"

She replied:

Never! I always believed that I was capable of winning, but in a competition like pageantry as well as many other sports, the fastest runner doesn't necessarily win the race. There are always extenuating circumstances. My husband said to me, 'Can you really quit now when you came so close? You know this isn't just about going out there and winning the Super Bowl trophy, this is about getting out there and having the guts to dive for the pass.'

I asked her, "Where did you find the courage to try again and why *did* you ultimately decide to return in 2008?" And her answer was:

In November of 2007, my husband, John, at the age of forty-two suffered a massive heart attack. After almost losing him I realized how quickly life can be taken from us. How the words, 'live every day as if it were your last' suddenly made so much sense.

I knew I wanted to be Mrs. Colorado and I knew that I was right for the job. The idea of sitting in the audience and watching someone else win the crown was too much for me to take. It took months of soul searching to realize that it would be far worse to sit in the audience and watch someone else achieve my dream than to stand on stage and be a part of the pageant. At least if I tried, there was a chance I would win. I knew that I had truly come to a point that it wasn't just about getting out there and winning that Super Bowl trophy, but about having the guts to play in the big game. I was going to dive for that winning touchdown pass as if it were the last game I would ever play.

"Come prepared to play the best game of your life and be ready to dive for the pass! You never know—you might just catch the ball!"
~ Christina Sacha – Mrs. Colorado 2008

Do you look to others for the nod of approval? Do you solicit the opinion of people before deciding to go out on a limb and try something new? Are *your* self-defeating thoughts robbing you of your dreams/destiny? Or worse yet, is someone else's negativity holding you back? If you've answered yes to any of these questions you may want to reflect inward and look upward for the courage to *believe* that you can.

When I competed my third year for the Mrs. Colorado title and crown I wasn't sure that my family was *fully* on board with my decision, however, I couldn't let the dream die. I didn't want to look back on my life and realize I had lived in a world of *what ifs*, so without much trepidation I entered again and went for the crown.

Directors get asked a lot of random questions and we usually have answers. However, there was one question I couldn't answer, or moreover *refused* to answer, and that was: "Tricia, do *you* think I can win?"

And I always responded, "It doesn't matter what I think, the only thing that really matters is that *you* believe you can!"

Faith – The Power Of Believing That You Can

The Take Away

- Rely on self-belief not that of others.
- Bolster the belief in yourself with hard work and determination.
- Dismiss nagging, toxic self-doubt as counterproductive.
- Don't solicit the opinions of negative people when it comes to the topic of your dreams.

Amy Nugent – Mrs. Colorado 1996

Chapter Five

Be Fearless — Not Reckless

"Courage is the discovery that you may not win,
and trying when you know you can lose."
~ Tom Krause – Motivational Speaker

If you were to ask me to list the top five most influential people in my life, I could easily identify the top three. First my mother and father and not necessarily in that order, they both contributed equally, but in *very* different ways. The third person was a girl named Desiree Graham.

It was about the third week into my eighth grade year, my sixth school to date, and I hadn't made a friend yet, not even an acquaintance. In those days, I waited for people to seek me out. I hadn't connected the dots that if I wanted to make friends, I needed to be a little more proactive. I accidentally stumbled upon a scuffle in the girls' bathroom, nothing serious, but amidst the elevated voices a girl pointed at me and said, "I'm walking home with *you!*" I shrugged my shoulders and meekly replied, "Okay."

That was the beginning of a friendship that would forever change my junior high status, and more importantly, it was the dawning of a new personal perspective. Just to fill you in, Desiree was *everything* I was not; she was spontaneous, funny, high-spirited and above all else she was fearless. By the end of that year, she looked at me and said, "We're trying out for the pom-pom squad." I must have had a look of colossal panic on my face—I told her she was crazy, after all I was the *new* kid and *shy* on top of it, not necessarily top qualifications for becoming a member of a cheer team. But it didn't matter because she signed us up for the competition anyway. So I humored her, what could it hurt?

We worked really hard on our optional routines; practicing every night in her backyard, and to this day, I still remember the words to my cheer and the first sixteen counts of choreography:

We're out to win... (clap, clap) so let's begin... (clap, clap)
By giving a cheer... (clap, clap) for all to hear... (clap, clap)

On the day of try-outs, fifty girls showed up for seven positions and we were required to audition in alphabetical order. Since my maiden name was Woods, you guessed it, I was number fifty. I had to anxiously sit and watch forty-nine other girls try-out before I got my chance.

On the exterior, I wasn't exactly the "poster girl" for self-confidence, but what I *can* say about myself was that I wasn't afraid of failure. I wasn't afraid to try because I might not win. What a blessing! And even though I entered the competition only to humor my best friend, I admit that by the time I got in front of the judges, I *really* wanted to win. Many a night I fell asleep practicing that cheer in my head and imagined what it would be like to wear the blue and gold uniform of a Broomfield Junior High Viking pom-pom girl.

It took about an hour for the judges to tally the scores while all fifty of us junior high girls bounced off the walls of the gymnasium with nervous anticipation. Upon reflection, I'm not sure that I remember what was going through my mind. I don't really think I *expected* to win, but I know I hadn't ruled it out either. Nevertheless, sixty minutes later the results were announced and a delirious Tricia Woods had indeed landed a position on the B.J.H.S. pom-pom squad. But unfortunately, my high spirited, spontaneous partner-in-crime, Desiree, did not.

Later, my mother told me that she just assumed Desiree was a shoo-in and thought that I would have struggled to keep up with her. Apparently my *own* mother thought I was really reaching, and sadly I agreed with her. The good news is that Desiree and I remained best friends throughout high school and she continued celebrating my later successes in competition. Desiree had taught me the invaluable lesson of being fearless.

Even though I was the new kid, even though I was shy by nature, and even though I had never had any formal training in dance, I dared to step outside my comfort zone and try something new. Undoubtedly, the process was easier as a pre-teen, but I've witnessed many grown women exhibit the same fearless attitude when signing up to compete in their first pageant and in some instances their very *first* competition of any sort.

As the director, in my consultation appointments and monthly newsletters, I felt it was my goal to generate excitement and energize my contestants to *want* to win; in other words, to get everyone pumped up. And oddly enough the response I quite often got was unexpected, "I don't want to get *too* excited, in case I don't win."

What? Are you serious?

To me this attitude was akin to practicing disappointment. I'm pretty sure that by the time we advance from kindergarten to first grade most of us have experienced some form of defeat. Why suppress enthusiasm for your dreams because you fear falling short of your expectations?

I'm absolutely sure that nobody has ever died from the disappointment of not winning a pageant. I told them in no uncertain terms that their fear of disappointment was total nonsense. My theory was, if you don't win, go to the nearest Italian restaurant with your supporters, and order a glass of wine and a large pepperoni pizza. (If you don't drink order a banana split instead.) Before the night is over the camaraderie and laughs will be enough to soothe a disappointed spirit. Well… at least it always worked for me.

So how does reckless fit into this equation? Being fearless is a fine quality if it's not coupled with being reckless. The best example I can think of would be a person who decides to embark on climbing his or her first fourteener without having a game-plan to make it to the top. An experienced climber would physically build up his or her stamina with some endurance training, pack the appropriate gear, wear standard hiking boots, and prepare for the "unexpected" like inclement weather or maybe even a run-in with menacing wildlife. In other words if you want to take on a challenge, it pays to be fearless, but if you want to make it to the top, don't recklessly begin without the proper planning.

Over the years, I encountered women who recklessly signed up for the pageant weeks before the final deadline without proper preparation. I'm not necessarily making an issue out of a short preparation timeline, as there are a lot of tenacious people who can make things happen quickly, but they are usually well aware of the resources and energy that it will require to make it happen. Rather, I'm addressing the contestant who has flirted with the idea of competing for months, perused the website, requested the entry information and has perhaps spent a lot of time *daydreaming* about the possibility of entering instead of using the time to actually prepare. Time forces her hand and she finally enters, but now faces real challenges at making a successful bid for the title. Usually these women would be the *most* discouraged when it was all over. I'm convinced that with the proper preparation these "reckless" contestants would have stood a real chance of winning, or at the very least placing, but because they didn't have the positive experience that they had hoped for they never bothered to try again.

This same phenomenon applied to some repeat contestants who, for whatever reason, procrastinated until the last minute to sign up. It gave us very little time to work up a new game plan to make changes based on their prior performance. If you're going to compete, give yourself enough time to be competitive.

One of the frequently asked questions to appear on the Mrs. Colorado website was: Can a first-timer win the pageant? The answer is yes! In the combined twenty years I spent competing and directing I saw it happen four times in just our system alone. So I made a point of studying these four titleholders to find out what they might have in common. Two of them had prior pageant experience as single women, so I ruled them out as possible "fearless" contestants. The other two had never entered a pageant before and didn't come from competitive backgrounds. However, they both did have some performance experience, i.e., singing or modeling.

One of them was Amy Nugent who entered the pageant in 1996. It was her first pageant competition and her main objective for entering was to overcome her fear of public speaking. Talk about fearless; this to me was like jumping into the ocean to overcome the fear of water.

As I mentioned she had some performance experience as a singer. She visited with me in her preparation session, asked a lot of questions, took notes and applied the advice that was being offered. She had entered in plenty of time to do her research, her homework and bring her A-game to the pageant.

In 1996, our competition structure included a top ten question. In this category of judging, I personally created a unique question for each participant based on information submitted from her biography form. When the top ten were announced, the accountant pulled the questions from a file and handed them directly to me with the tally sheet.

Amy's question that year was: "I see that you're a singer; if your life was a country western song what would it be and why?" She took the microphone, turned to the audience and gave a brief description of the song *Every Day Now* and a short profile of the songwriter, Chuck Pile. She then asked me if she could sing a couple of bars. Taken a little off guard, I gave her a nod of the head, and she brought the house down by singing the rest of her answer.

Besides being attractive and obviously talented, Amy was fearless! She had the courage to stand out by trying something different, but something that was well within the range of her abilities. She may have been fearless, but she was not reckless.

As I got to know her in the coming year she confessed to being surprised that she had made it to the top five. She recounts that just before the fourth runner-up was named she thought, *what an honor it is to be the fourth runner-up among such incredible competitors*. Still clapping for the other participants, she thought, *wow I can't believe I've placed as high as third runner-up*. Then in total disbelief, she couldn't imagine that she had actually made it all the way to the position of second runner-up.

Every time she would tell the story to someone new, I found myself laughing. One day I interrupted and asked, "So when *did* you honestly think, Gee I might have actually *won* this thing?" And she replied, "Not until I heard my name called." Amy was fearless and humble, both great attributes of a real winner.

Unfortunately there are countless opportunities to be reckless in pageant competition. Besides not allowing enough time to prepare, there are those contestants who conversely complete their preparations with time to spare. In this short span of time, these women begin to second guess their decisions. Or maybe, they're not comfortable with being "ready" and for some reason it feels good to continue making changes. Changes that were *not* necessary.

One such woman, returned for a second shot at the title after not having placed at all the prior year. She diligently worked to make all the necessary adjustments to ensure success. She worked out, bought the right gown, studied interview techniques, and submitted beautiful photographs, showcasing her friendly smile and shoulder-length, golden blonde hair. However, just days before the competition something possessed her to cut her hair in a very short, spiky style and color it auburn red with chunky blonde highlights.

When I first saw her I *couldn't* pretend that I didn't notice the dramatic change. When I asked her why she did it, she replied, "I thought I would go punky." I wanted to scream, "What are you thinking, the words *punky* and *pageantry* don't belong in the same sentence," but instead I just smiled before I turned and walked away. Besides being contrary to the "right look" for the competition she had entered, she now no longer looked like her photo in the program book. I was so disappointed for her because in one fell swoop she had made a reckless choice and there was no way to fix it!

Early in my directorship, I had a dear, dear contestant who had competed for several years always making it into the top five. Armed with a couple years of experience and a competitive evening gown, I believed she was on target to give it her best shot ever. Two months before the pageant she queried me about having her bust line surgically enhanced. I *strongly* advised her against it. It was just the wrong decision for so many reasons. I'll discuss my philosophy on pageantry and plastic surgery at greater length in another chapter, but for the sake of this argument, I didn't believe that a larger bust measurement was going to give her a competitive edge. In fact, I've never seen a bust line win a pageant, but rather it's the skilled competitor who wins! I argued that the beautiful dress she had worked so hard to buy would probably not fit, thus causing her another quandary in the final weeks before competition. And lastly, but *most* importantly, her body would not have enough time to fully recover, affecting not only her sense of well-being, but her energy level as well.

But, alas, she didn't take my advice. She recklessly had the surgery, the gown no longer fit and she physically had a hard time making it through the long rehearsals and competition. Well, thankfully she didn't regret having the surgery, she was happy with her new look, but I genuinely feel that the timing of the decision was bad and probably cost her the opportunity to win.

These are two fairly dramatic examples of reckless decision making, but I saw it happen every year in much smaller ways, like giving creative autonomy to make-up artists and hair stylists. Or one of my personal favorites is the contestant who makes a conscious decision during the *actual* competition to change up her choreography from that which had been taught and practiced in rehearsals. She, for no apparent reason, just decides to do her own thing and ends up looking like the wedding guest who after one too many drinks needs to be hauled off the dance floor.

Stay focused and be fearless in the pursuit of your dreams, but be wise in the direction you take to get there.

Be Fearless - Not Reckless

The Take Away

- Be fearless—put your dreams into motion.
- Make sure you have allowed enough time to learn and properly prepare.
- Be enthusiastic about your goals.
- Remember that mentally preparing for defeat before the competition has even begun is a dangerous form of self-sabotage.
- Making reckless last minute changes on the home stretch of preparation can have a deleterious affect on your success.

Debi Moore – Mrs. Colorado 1994

Chapter Six

Be The Original
God Created You To Be

"Today you are You, that is truer than true.
There is no one alive who is Youer than You."

~ Dr. Seuss – American Writer and Cartoonist

There's a fine line between being original and adhering to the guidelines of the competition as outlined in the first chapter, "Understand The Game You Are Playing," but the distinction needs to be drawn. Boxers, golfers and tennis players all wear the same basic uniform and perform the same skills needed to compete in their respective sports, but each player still brings uniqueness to their games through style and execution. Pageant competition is no different. Competitors are asked to compete in very specific categories, but it's the individual who doesn't abandon her originality who usually stands out in the crowd.

We're all uniquely coded to be original by way of our DNA, but unfortunately we spend most of our lives trying to be like everybody else. I totally blame the junior high/middle school experience for this *fit-in-at-all-cost* disorder that robs us of our personal authenticity. And since my school experience was complicated by several out of state moves, I struggled with the idea of being *true to myself* well into adulthood.

I grew up wanting to be just like Denise Fink; by far the most popular girl at Broomfield Junior High School and who was hands down the obvious choice for Homecoming Queen of the 1975 graduating senior class. Granted she was a fine girl to want to emulate, but hey, I was *never* going to be Denise—I was Tricia. Too bad I didn't realize the value of authenticity much sooner. I'm pleased to say that I'm still good friends with Denise. She's every bit as wonderful today as she was in junior high, but now I'm happy to let her be Denise and only ask of myself to be the best "Tricia" I can manage.

Originality Doesn't Always Equate To Being Extraordinary Or Profound

When I first entered the Mrs. Colorado Pageant, I was all about defining the game. I was good at watching the televised pageants and translating the information into competition, but all I was doing was mimicking winning behavior. During my first year in 1987, the contestants were all asked to fill out a stage form that provided the emcee with information to read during the various competitions. One of the questions was, "What is your husband's favorite recipe?" So I made the mistake of actually asking my husband instead of just filling out the paperwork on my own. He responded with, "I like your chicken-chili."

To which I blustered, "I'm not saying 'chicken-chili,' that sounds too average—too ordinary—too unimaginative."

And he came back with, "That's it. That's my favorite dish, your chicken-chili."

He won the debate. Chicken-chili—final answer! You see, I didn't want to say chicken-chili because I didn't think it sounded good enough. I wanted to sound like an incredible cook; which I wasn't. In fact I'm a terrible cook, but I'm pretty good at using the crock-pot. Seriously—like being a good cook was going to give me an extra edge in the competition. Now I'm fairly confident, if not down right positive, that if culinary skills were required to win the Mrs. Colorado crown the organizers would have included a cook-off.

Since winning the Mrs. Colorado title in 1989, I've been invited to judge a lot of pageants including many teen competitions. This same phenomenon exists there as well. The teens were almost always asked something akin to, "What do you want to be when you grow up?" And you can't believe how many kids aspire to be pediatricians and attorneys. After hearing it a gazillion times, it was so refreshing when a competitor would say, "Gee I'm not sure yet, but beauty school sounds fun." Now don't get me wrong, I'm not suggesting that teens shouldn't dream about becoming doctors and lawyers, what I'm pointing out is that the candor of the delegate who considered a career in beauty school was positively authentic and the judges knew it.

When Originality Collides With Trend

The '80s mentality of *bigger is better* applied to just about everything in life including hair styles. Back then I had pretty hair; it was long and silky, but it was *not* big. So I, along with most American women, permed my hair to make it as big as I could get it. During my competition years my mother used to tell me, "Why don't you wear your hair up or back off of your face?" She went on to explain that she felt it best showcased my facial features. *Well, I would have none of that!* After all what did *she* know; she was just my mother?

During the 1989 national Mrs. America Pageant I was standing next to Mrs. Oklahoma in the dressing room. Just minutes before we were all about to compete in the preliminary round of swimsuit competition she became frustrated with trying to make her hair look big, so she decided on something different and far more befitting of her personal style. I'll never forget what she said next. She was sort of addressing those standing around her, but mostly just talking out loud when she exclaimed, "My director's going to kill me." And with that she pulled her hair back into a low ponytail. I thought, *whoa, that's a really bold move*—big hair was in and all. Mrs. Oklahoma, Jennifer Johnson, went on to become Mrs. America 1989!

Jennifer was a beautiful and talented woman who didn't need big hair to be a standout; she decided to do what worked best for her and that authenticity turned out to be the perfect choice.

Originality And Following Competition Guidelines Are Not Opposing Concepts

I always worked really hard to provide my state titleholders with wardrobe and resources to make them as competitive as possible at the national pageant, but I most prided myself on giving them my time and direction. It was the one thing I felt was missing in my bid for the national title, so I wanted to make sure that all of my representatives felt informed, coached and emotionally supported at every turn. After all, someone should benefit from the lessons I learned via the mistakes that I had made. I was involved in just about every aspect of their preparations from shopping and photo shoots to helping them fill out their paperwork and booking appearances that would boost their public speaking ability.

In 1994, only three years into my career as a pageant director, I was driving the newly crowned Mrs. Colorado, Debi Moore, to a photo shoot. We didn't know each other very well and I found myself trying to make small talk on the way to the studio. I told her in passing that she was going to love the make-up artist that was sponsoring her services and that the make-up application was so perfect she wouldn't be able to see so much as a freckle. To which she replied, "But I like my freckles."

I probably gave her an eye-roll, but that conversation really struck me and in some ways it was probably responsible for a shift in my thinking. By then I had only sent two women to the national pageant. My first titleholder in 1992, Janet Horvath, was a forty-year-old nurse anesthetist, wife of a doctor, who had spent years competing in the world of natural bodybuilding. She was highly educated and had a very strong sense of self.

One year later, Debbie Barnhill took home the title. She was half Japanese and half European/Caucasian. Her beauty was exotic and her personality was charming, humble and soft spoken.

Debi Moore, my third titleholder, was twenty-four years old and a very simple, genuine country girl. She was the quintessential *All-American-girl-next-door*. She was very different from my first two titleholders and the problem was that I hadn't yet become a seasoned director. I was trying to fit all three of them into the "beauty queen mold" instead of capitalizing on their distinctive qualities.

That casual conversation about make-up and freckles had shed light on the fact that I wasn't treating my delegates as individuals and a course correction was eventually made. And in the end, I think I got really good at being able to help my contestants *and* titleholders nurture their individuality, while teaching them the ropes of competition.

Borrowed Originality Really Isn't Original

There's a saying in the pageant industry that goes like this: "Crown chasers and copycats don't win pageants." I always thought it sounded a little judgmental, but the next story illustrates the validity of this old adage.

Many state directors will judge each other's competitions. Of course you only invite those directors who you feel have your best interests at heart. In the spring of 2009, I was invited to judge one such competition. It's always fun to see the way my colleagues produce a pageant. The competition and the contestant in this story shall remain nameless to protect personal feelings.

It was a great show that included an opening production number where all of the contestants were asked to come up with a costume that she thought best represented her state: much like the national competition. The costumes were elaborate, brightly colored and ingenious. Each contestant had to introduce themselves and describe their costume, at both the preliminary and final competitions. I was enjoying the extravaganza and even though we were not asked to formally judge the contestants in costume, I listened closely to every word spoken and paid close attention to the detail that had gone into each creation.

By the finals night, I was fairly positive that I had already decided on my top three over-all candidates based on their performance during the preliminary round. As the production began I sat back in my seat ready to take in all of the splendor and excitement. But something funny happened and I wasn't the only judge who noticed it.

At the last minute, one of my top three choices for the title decided to change up her original introduction from the night before. She "coincidentally" ended her introduction with the same, very clever opening line of the contestant who immediately followed her. It threw the other contestant for a loop, sending the poor woman into a stammering mess. In all fairness, I don't think "Contestant A" took the line to hurt "Contestant B," but rather, I think she copied the line because she thought it sounded good. However, she obviously had failed to think through the unintended consequences of her actions. Not only was she guilty of being blatantly unoriginal, but her decision had caused someone else to stumble; thus casting herself in an unfavorable light.

The sad thing was that "Contestant A" didn't need to copy anything; she was already a standout for a lot of reasons. She *did* place in the top five as I had predicted earlier, but when asked to place the contestants in an exact order on the final ballot, I placed her in the last position based on her actions in the costume competition. She went from being one of my top three contenders for the title to ultimately my choice for last place.

How To Explain The Concept Of Originality

I spent years answering questions like:

- Do most women win with their hair up or down?
- Should I wear a white gown, because it seems like a lot of contestants win in white?

And my favorite question of all:

- What do the judges *want* to hear in the interview?

I think these women thought there was a *top secret* formula for success and that pageant insiders were less than forthcoming with the information. In fact there *is* a formula for success and here it is: Conform to the standards of the competition you have selected without forfeiting the very essence of who you are!

Here are the top secret answers to the three most frequently asked questions:

- Choose to wear your hair in a style or fashion that best showcases *your* features.
- Your gown should be *spectacular*, but the color does *not* determine the winner. A lot of competitors win in white because a lot of competitors wear white; that's the simple fact. It's just about the numbers.
- The judges want to know who *you* are! Trust me, even the most naïve, unseasoned judge can spot the perfectly rehearsed canned answers and almost always find them to be boring if not completely uninspired.

My best advice: explore your God-given uniqueness and move forward with the confidence that it's not only good enough to win, but it's absolutely essential to winning.

Be The Original God Created You To Be

The Take Away

- Resist the urge to sound and look like someone you're not.
- Believe that being real is good enough.
- Be careful when defining the game you are playing to be mindful of your individuality.
- Don't look for ways to be like someone else, instead look for ways to be a standout based on your own uniqueness.

Jennifer Lamont – Mrs. Colorado 2005

Chapter Seven

Choose To Inspire Those Around You

"If your actions inspire others to dream more, learn more, do more and become more, you are a leader."
~ John Quincy Adams – Sixth President of the United States

I believe competition challenges most people to seek and obtain personal growth, but it also offers us the unique opportunity to be an inspiration to others.

In January 2001, my husband, Russell, ran a half marathon in Las Vegas. After completing that run he believed with the proper training he could finish the 26.2 miles required of a full marathon. So he bought a book on how to train and signed up for the 2003 race in Maui, Hawaii. At mile eighteen in training he injured himself and his dream of running the Maui Marathon was lost; the injury required months of abstinence from any form of exercise. I thought maybe this would be the end of his new found interest in running, but much to my surprise, in January 2005, he announced that he had been selected from a random lottery to run in the prestigious New York Marathon. His dream was still alive; he started training again, but this time he incorporated more stretching into his regimen and did a better job of pacing himself.

In November of that year, nearly four years since first deciding to compete, Russell and approximately forty-five thousand other runners began their quest for the "Finisher's Medal." He had purchased a ticket for me to stand at the finish line with hundreds of other ramped-up relatives and friends. (It was truly incredible, but insane.) When I got to the bleachers I was so worried he wouldn't see me, that every time a seat was vacated I moved closer and closer to the barricades until finally a spot in the front miraculously opened up and I squeezed my way in. I was so excited; he was now due to cross in approximately three hours.

The waves of human drama that unfolded before me over the next several hours were amazing. Soon after securing my position next to the barricade, the first two elite runners appeared running side by side as they approached the finish line. The crowd went wild—one of these two men would be the first of forty-five thousand people to finish the race and take home the grand prize and a place in marathon history. It looked as though it would be a photo finish when one of the runners stretched his neck to cross the finish line first. He lost his balance and fell! We all drew a collective breath and then together exhaled a collective groan. It was truly hard to reconcile the ultimate joy of one man while watching the other man pick himself up to stagger across the finish line still brushing the gravel lodged in his skin.

That day, I witnessed the indomitable human spirit. A man with no legs on a skateboard had done the 26.2 miles on his knuckles, some people near exhaustion literally crawled across the finish line, people in wheelchairs crossed, father/son teams crossed, team Louisiana (all survivors of the 2005 hurricane Katrina) crossed, and then finally in the sea of faces, I saw him. There was my Russell sporting the biggest smile. When I yelled out his name, he ran over to give me a kiss then crossed the finish line. He collected his prized New York Marathon Finisher's Medal nearly four years after he first began his training.

But the most emotional moment of the entire race came hours later

project. The assignment called for him to make a poster of his life with a category that included "my hero." There on his poster board was a picture of Roni. When she asked him, "Why did you pick me to be your hero?" He replied, "Because you inspire me to be a better person."

So whether you're the last place finisher in a marathon who unknowingly touched the lives of a couple from Colorado, a woman who defied her age to enter a state pageant that included a swimsuit competition and generated unbelievable enthusiasm from an entire audience, or simply a grandmother who refused to quit because she didn't want to send the wrong message to an impressionable little boy, we all have the power to be influential to someone, somewhere, at sometime. I hope you choose to inspire!

Choose To Inspire Those Around You

The Take Away

- As you contemplate competing ask yourself: If I could serve as a role model to someone I didn't know what would I want to be remembered for?
- Will your actions during preparation *and* competition serve as an inspiration to those around you?
- Reflect on someone in your life who has inspired you and ask the question: What was it that he or she possessed that made him or her an inspiration?
- Ask yourself: How will adopting an inspirational attitude actually help me realize my own goals?

Marney Duckworth – Mrs. Colorado 2006

Chapter Eight

Learn From Your Experience

*"Experience is the hardest teacher because it gives
a test first and the lessons afterwards."*
~ Lindsay Thomas – Motivational Speaker

After the annual pageant competition, some participants tried to make an issue out of the fact that many of our titleholders were re-peat contestants; like they somehow got extra credit for entering more than once. I could sum up my response to these women in one word. *Experience!* I then followed the statement with a question: "If you took up tennis tomorrow would you plan to win Wimbledon by the end of the year?" I usually only posed the question to defensive contestants and most of the time all I got from the question was silence. I never had much patience for people who just wanted to grumble about their loss when there was obvious room for improvement. Of course, experience isn't worth much unless you learn from it. If you don't benefit by learning from your experiences then you are just clocking time on this planet.

In the late '70s, I decided to try out for The Pony Express (the professional cheerleaders for the Denver Broncos football team). That weekend over seven hundred fifty women auditioned for the team and by late Sunday afternoon, I had auditioned a whopping eighteen times, modeled a casual outfit of my choice, and given a personal interview for the panel of judges. I was ultimately cut at number seventy-five. I was tired *and* disappointed, but I was young and there was always next year. I walked away that weekend and never made an assessment as to why I got cut when I got cut. Unfortunately "next year" never came; the Broncos organization decided to eliminate professional cheerleaders from their program indefinitely.

I got a second chance when in the early '80s Denver was awarded a franchise in the USFL spring football league, which included a professional dance team. By then I was in my mid-twenties and felt that maybe I was verging on aging out, but I decided to go for it anyway. I competed with over three hundred fifty women for a position on the squad and by the end of the day I got cut at number fifty.

At this point it was impossible to ignore the coincidence that I kept getting cut at approximately the same number in the audition process. I finally did what I should have done years earlier. I made a personal assessment as to what I was missing. I looked around at the women who were advancing to the final round and the reason was ridiculously obvious. Most, if not all, of the finalists had a strong background in dance. In fact many of them had been dancing all of their lives. With each audition and as the field narrowed, I found myself struggling to learn the new choreography. I had a lot of experience as a cheerleader, but this was a different game; this position required high level dance skills. So I immediately entered myself in an advanced dance class and took private lessons with the intentions of trying out again the following year. The effort was well worth it and I landed a spot on the 1985 Pure Gold dance team. Cheering for a professional sports team was all that I had imagined it to be. For me, it was that once in a lifetime opportunity to be a part of something really big and I truly enjoyed every minute of the season, including the challenge of keeping up with very accomplished dancers.

Learning from experience was instinctive to Marney Duckworth, a natural born competitor who grew up thriving through competition. As a child she competed in 4-H for over ten years, winning the 1987 "Grand Champion Market Steer" which is apparently the *piece de resistance* of awards at the county fair. She held records in high school basketball, volleyball, and also ran track & field. She was state champion in speech two years running, and was crowned Miss Nebraska Teen USA in 1992. She went on to play college basketball on a full-ride scholarship and continued competing and placing in both the Miss Nebraska America and USA systems for a couple of years. I only list her background and achievements so that you can grasp the nature of her competitive spirit.

I vividly remember the day I met Marney. There was something about her that I found hard to describe. I just knew she possessed rare qualities that would surely catapult her to success. She first competed for the Mrs. Colorado title in 2005, placed second runner-up and won both the "Most Photogenic" and "Best in Interview" awards. At the time, her son, Owen, was only eight months old and she had worked hard that year to get back into shape so quickly after his birth.

She decided to compete again the following year and in our personal appointment she asked me, "So *what do* I need to do to win?" I knew by the way she asked the question that she was serious and wanted an honest answer. If you're going to ask that question then you had better be prepared to hear the truth.

I hesitated for a moment grappling for the right approach. I told her that she needed to lose about eight more pounds and that she needed to work on the delivery of the dreaded "final question." She took the critique with grace. It's not easy hearing that you need to lose weight and it's certainly not easy being the one who has to deliver the message.

I hated to tell women that they needed to get into better shape and usually in most cases I would only elude to the fact by suggesting that they might find it valuable to work with a nutritionist and or a personal trainer. In Marney's case, I felt that she was not only willing to hear the truth, but was also capable of processing my assessment without becoming defensive; a key quality in serious competitors.

It was late fall and the holidays were fast approaching. I was never big on setting unrealistic goals for my contestants so I suggested that she wait until January before attempting a diet. I will never forget what she said next, "I've had thirty years to eat whatever I wanted to eat at Christmas—so I'm pretty sure it won't kill me to diet *this* year." On May 20, 2006, Marney Duckworth, once again, won the "Best in Interview" award and this time captured the Mrs. Colorado title and crown.

After she won, we met the following week to begin preparations for the national Mrs. America Pageant. She asked me if I would mind working with her at least once a week, specifically on interview. I found it curious as to why she would want to continue working on communication skills; after all she had won the "Best in Interview" award two years in a row and this year had done a sensational job of answering her final question. It was then that I had a glimpse into the heart of a true competitor because instead of assuming that she had reached the top of her game, she believed that there was still room to improve.

We had a great summer. While I always made myself available to work with every Mrs. Colorado titleholder, not all of them felt they needed additional training. I really had fun working with the ones who had a competition background because generally they were the most coachable. Just because you win once doesn't mean by any stretch of the imagination that you've reached the pinnacle of your game. I believe real learning comes in increments. After all, even world class athletes continue to work with coaches.

That year the Mrs. Colorado organization had become involved with a residential and continuum of care services facility for young girls. These precious children for various reasons could not be placed in foster care. It was, in effect, a modern day orphanage for pre-teens and teens. Marney was scheduled to make an appearance to tour the facility and visit with the residents. I decided to tag along because I'd been in serious talks with the director of the program about a high level of involvement between our two organizations.

The facility caretakers, or house mothers, expressed their reservations about the girls being exposed to a "beauty queen" who appeared to live a charmed life. Perhaps the house moms were guilty of buying into the T.V. commercial stereotype that pageant titleholders are pretty robotrons only famous for riding in convertibles, waving the hand-cupped "pageant wave" in small town parades. Or maybe they were fearful of the myth that pageant titleholders are self-indulgent beauties with no substance, who arrogantly project the notion—*wouldn't it be nice to be me*. Of course that was never our attitude or approach to community service, but I understood their apprehension nonetheless.

Marney had obtained her teaching degree along with a Masters in Technology and Learning and had taught school in the inner city, so she had some experience relating to troubled kids. She bought them all brightly colored note pads and pencils and during her visit asked them to make a list of their goals and dreams; the things they most wanted in life. She then asked them to put their notepads aside and relayed a personal story of a goal she had set for herself in high school. Here is a selected passage of that talk:

My dad ran hurdles in high school and I thought that I might be good at it too, since speed plus long legs is generally a good combination. After training with the coach for the track and field team I ran my heart out at the first meet and came in last place.

I have always believed that you can try harder—work harder at everything. I knew I was athletic enough to do it; I just needed to focus and train harder. But what really drove me was another chance to prove whether or not I could do it. I love to compete. I love to win. I couldn't expect to get better by just putting in the regular track practice after school with everyone else. I had to put in extra time after practice and on the weekends as well.

Overall my time improved—I can't say that I ran any faster, but I learned breathing techniques and most importantly a strategy for actually running the race. I learned that the race wasn't just about hearing the gun go off and running for your life or jumping over hurdles as you encountered them. (Oh, and hoping you didn't die before hitting the finish line.)

I actually learned that I needed to know how many strides were between each hurdle during the race, so that I could pace myself. And, if I ever got off stride, what I needed to do to compensate for it before getting to the next hurdle. So much about the 300 meter hurdles is about surviving. I've seen some of the fastest people not win the race because they didn't have a plan on how they would actually run it.

I worked hard and I improved, at least I wasn't last place—but I never won a 300 meter hurdles race.

As I sat and listened to her presentation, I couldn't help but wonder why she chose to talk to these young teens about her failure rather than one of her many successes. She continued to ask them about their lists and encouraged them to share their future dreams with the group. She also challenged them to write down the things that they could do now to begin working toward their goals.

Later when we had the chance to sit down and talk about the day, I asked her why she had decided to talk about the 300 meter hurdles over her standing records in basketball. She told me, "I knew going into this appearance that their lives weren't easy, but I wanted them to know that it doesn't have to stay that way. I wanted them to know I had failed."

Over the years, in one of many personal conversations with Marney, we talked about her competitive nature and philosophized on why some people are more competitive than others. I asked her if her parents had made a conscious effort to teach these principles. She wasn't sure, but she did tell me this:

I'd come home from a basketball game that we had just won. My father and I would sit down at the kitchen table and talk about how it could have been better. Don't get me wrong, there was plenty of celebrating, but we never missed an opportunity to learn where I could have improved my game.

This is the perfect example of learning from critique. She could have easily looked at her father and said, "Geez Dad, we *won*, why are you pointing out what I could have done better?"

After several years of giving real, honest evaluation to contestants after the pageant, I learned that not everyone wanted to hear the truth even when presented with the utmost diplomacy. I began to fine tune the art of discernment. I learned to ask questions that might lead a jilted competitor to her own conclusion rather than serving up the facts unadulterated. And then there were a small number of angry, self-defeated contestants who just wanted to spew disappointment and blame. For those women I just gave them the outlet that they so desperately needed, but I assure you they never learned a thing from me—I just gave them the opportunity to vent.

As a competitor, I was just the opposite. I wanted to hear it in plain English. Don't dance around the truth, just give me the facts. Not to say that it didn't send a twinge of "ouch" through my psyche, but it was better to feel the temporary sting of critique than to struggle to find answers that probably didn't exist in my personal knowledge base.

Many pageant directors are not willing to give their competitors feedback because of the verbally abusive reactions of a handful of short-sighted contestants. To them it's just not worth it. However, I think this policy is unjust to the approximately ninety percent who really wanted to learn from their experience, so I forged ahead and gave everyone in my competition the opportunity to have a personal, post-pageant phone consultation.

I competed for the 1989 Mrs. America title in Las Vegas, and after seventeen days of tapings, rehearsals and preliminary competition, the top ten semi-finalists were announced. I was not among them. The last thing I saw before the curtain went down on the forty remaining state delegates was my mother, hands clasped and teary eyed. I asked one of our chaperones to deliver her a note that said, "I'm okay, enjoy the show."

I never shed a tear that night and I'm pleased I didn't. It's not the way I wanted to be remembered by the "Class of 1989." Don't get me wrong, I did suffer some personal angst in the following weeks to come. Now remember, I'm the *if-I-can-do-it-three-times-girl*, I can win it! But Mrs. America was a once in a lifetime shot! I couldn't try again even if I could have competed in another state. Later, after becoming a director, I, along with many of my colleagues, lobbied the Mrs. America organization to change that particular rule. They didn't and in hindsight, I now believe it was the right decision.

The *finality* of the Mrs. America experience weighed heavy on my competitive heart. One morning before leaving for work, I was finishing up some routine tasks and I said out loud, "God, why not me—why not at least a placement in the top ten?" I paused for a moment as if to receive a divine memo right then and there, but I got no answer, not even in that *still small voice* that God is so famous for.

About five years into my directorship, I was conducting an orientation and I told the contestants, "Tonight when the pageant is over, when the winner has been chosen, when all the photos have been taken and the confetti is being swept from the stage, I will know how each and every one of you will feel. I've entered a pageant and placed—I've entered a pageant and won—and I've competed in a pageant and didn't make the first cut."

There was my epiphany and suddenly I heard that *still small voice,* "Tricia, that's why you didn't make the top ten at Mrs. America, because the lesson of your experience has shaped you to be a better director." By virtue of knowing exactly how each of them would feel I had the unique perspective to be a more compassionate and empathetic director. Now upon reflection, I wouldn't trade the lessons of that loss for the coveted 1989 Mrs. America title or that big, beautiful, rhinestone crown.

In the end, the real reward of loss, failure and disappointment is a chance to learn a lesson that can quite possibly transcend the competition you've entered and actually be applied elsewhere in life. Losing doesn't equate to failure, instead losing provides everyone who has an open-mind and a willing heart the opportunity to learn. Don't let the sting of failure rob you of the gratitude for the lessons you've learned along the way. And whatever you do, don't let it stop you from applying your experience and trying again!

Learn From Your Experience

The Take Away

- Ask yourself—what did I learn from this experience?
- Make an immediate assessment of your performance then give it two or three weeks and make a second personal evaluation; perhaps after you've had a chance to find some perspective through reviewing scores, viewing photos and watching the video or production telecast.
- Solicit the feedback from experts.
- Don't become defensive when critiqued. Look at constructive criticism as a learning tool, not a personal attack.
- Don't be afraid to apply the lessons you've learned and try again!
- Even in success remember to be coachable.

Paula Aurand – Mrs. Colorado 1995

Chapter Nine

Enjoy The Journey

"Success is a journey, not a destination.
The doing is often more important than the outcome."
~ Arthur Ashe – Professional Tennis Champion

I got hooked on the daytime drama, *All My Children* in high school, probably because my mother watched it every day while cleaning the house. In fact, the show was so popular in the '70s that college students actually arranged their course schedules around the timing of the show as not to miss an episode. The show's popularity among young people was largely due in part to the escapades of the complicated, gorgeous, trouble-maker, Erica Kane, played by the legendary Susan Lucci who in 1969 at the age of twenty-three years old, landed the role that is still considered by many critics to be one of the best roles on television written for women.

In 1978, Lucci received her first Daytime Emmy nomination. She was nominated again in 1981, and nominated almost every year since then. She became the first soap opera actress to appear on the cover of major magazines, as well as the first to star in Movies of the Week, but what made her a household name was her string of Emmy losses. It became a running joke that the "Queen of Daytime Television" had *no* crown but in 1999, on her *nineteenth* Emmy nomination, she won! She received a four minute standing ovation and now after twenty-one nominations, she is considered to be one of the most honored performers in the history of daytime television.

I think it's safe to say that on her "journey" to winning the coveted Emmy, Susan Lucci more than likely became discouraged and was probably tempted by self-doubt. As a devoted fan, I remember watching the 26th Annual Daytime Emmys and like many in the live audience, I was positively giddy with excitement for her. Ten years later as I watched it for the second time on YouTube, I once again found myself feeling emotional during her acceptance speech.

She began by saying, "Thank you so *very* much. I truly *never* believed that this would happen." The audience laughed. She goes on to thank the usual cast of characters like the writers, producers, co-workers, her parents and her husband, but what I found particularly poignant was when nearing the end of her acceptance speech she thanked her children, "To my children, to Liza and Andreas, I wasn't meant to get this award before tonight, because if I had, I wouldn't have that collection of poems—and letters—and drawings—and balloons—and chocolate cakes you made me all this time to make me feel better."

In other words, she would have missed out on the journey that made her victory so incredibly sweet! It's challenging to live in the present, and it's too bad that sometimes it's only while looking in the rearview mirror of life that we realize we did actually *enjoy the journey.*

Emily Stark first entered my pageant in 2000. She was a former Miss Colorado USA titleholder in 1995 and had judged the Mrs. Colorado competition for me that very same year. Given her pageant experience, I felt that she would prove to be very competitive. She placed in the top ten, but surprisingly failed to advance any further. She promised that she would come back, but that following year, she and her husband, James, decided to start a family and by the fall she was pregnant with twins.

Four months into her pregnancy the babies were diagnosed as conjoined. Immediately she and her husband literally faced gut-wrenching life and death decisions, beginning with the decision to continue with the pregnancy. A team of doctors advised them that eighty-five percent of pregnancies involving conjoined twins never make it to a live birth and out of the fifteen percent of live births only one out of every four survive the first twenty-four hours. For the Stark's there was never a question—the pregnancy would continue.

She successfully delivered the babies in March and the road to their separation began at once. I would occasionally hear how she was doing through the grapevine and followed her story in the media. That year, she and her sister came to the pageant in May and met me on stage to say hi once the production was over. I gave her a hug and feeling a bit uneasy about what I "should" say to her, I blurted out that I *did* indeed expect her to keep the promise to come back and compete. She laughed. But by early fall she had done just that, she signed up to compete in the 2002 pageant. I recall asking if the timing of her decision was good, given all that she faced. And her reply was an emphatic, "Yes!" When I interviewed her, years later, this is what she told me.

I'd been on an emotional rollercoaster for over a year and I honestly think that there was a span of months that I just couldn't find the time to shave my own legs. I was eighty pounds over weight and totally exhausted. I had become the third or fourth priority on my personal to-do list and in order to stay sane I needed something to look forward to. I viewed the Mrs. Colorado Pageant as a journey. It was a journey to find myself again. It was an opportunity to dress up, to feel and look beautiful and it came with a deadline set in stone to accomplish my weight loss goal. I wanted to put myself back together and I believed that this was a motivating way to do it.

In what can only be described as a fairytale ending, the twins were successfully separated without any permanent paralysis on October 9, 2001. Soon thereafter, Emily had scheduled her one-on-one appointment with me and when she arrived told me that she had left the hospital to make our meeting. I chided her, "*Emily*, we could have waited to do this at a more convenient time."

She replied, "No you don't understand, I've been sitting in a hospital for weeks, hour after hour and I just needed a break—the pageant gives me something to think about during these stressful days."

I finally got it. This wasn't just about winning, although I knew she wanted to win, winning wasn't her primary focus. This was also about finding the *joy in the journey* and Emily Stark *did* become Mrs. Colorado 2002.

Over time I collected letters, cards, and thank you notes from my pageant contestants. Upon occasion when I was experiencing a down day, I would rummage through the box and read a couple to lift my spirits. Here are excerpts from a handful of those letters describing what they found most valuable about their competition experience. They remind me of the Chinese proverb, "The *joy* is the reward."

"The pageant weekend was an experience I will cherish for a lifetime. The memories, friendships and stories have honestly made a place in my heart forever. It was exciting to reach the goals I set forth for myself and I left the pageant encouraged to set more. Before that weekend I thought I knew what to expect, but I never imagined I would leave feeling refreshed, encouraged, confident and connected to many other women."
~ Tracey Dinnel – Mrs. Colorado Springs 2002

"What an amazing experience! I'm going to try this again. I cannot believe all I've learned and how much more I want to learn."
~ Connie Patton – Mrs. Lincoln County 1999

"Thank you for the fantastic experience! What a great journey. I have grown spiritually and found out that I really can do anything I want if I put my mind to it!"
~ Marlene Berrier – Mrs. Pueblo West 2003

"You have no idea what a thrill it is to walk out on that stage at the Temple Buell Theatre and hear my friends and family cheering for me."
~ Melissa Ferris – Mrs. North Valley 2004

"A very big thank you for the awesome experience I gained in being a part of the Mrs. Colorado Pageant. For me, the excitement of being on stage, in the bright lights of the Ellie Caulkins Opera House was truly amazing. Looking out to four levels of audience members made me feel like a superstar."
~ Shelly Steele-Moorehead – Mrs. Frederick 2007

"At times my recovery (from a car accident) *is still very challenging and painful. I have used the motivation of the pageant to get through many difficult times. It also gives me courage to pursue things truly important to me. I'm taking care of myself even when I'm tired or busy and taking chances I didn't have the courage to take before I entered this pageant, to triumph over my injuries and the loss of time. I just never expected to see this kind of change in my life as a result of pageant preparation."*
~ Jessica Smith – Mrs. Lakewood 2007

*"I had a fabulous time and truly enjoyed myself. I want you
to know how fulfilled and rejuvenated I felt after spending
three whole days focused on me! I made some new friends
and hope my new relationships last a lifetime."*
~ Darcie Ell – Mrs. Loveland 2004

Inevitably re-reading these messages gave me time to reflect on the many outstanding women who participated in the pageant. Not only was I reminded of how they had benefited from the journey of competition, but that they truly enjoyed it as well.

There was a time in my life that I can honestly say I was *consumed* with the idea of "winning." So much so, that for years I know I missed opportunities to *enjoy the journey*, often times overlooking the biggest blessings that competition had to offer like the lessons of self-discovery, appreciation for the enduring support of family and friends, the thrill of dreaming and scheming, and the pure excitement of embarking upon a new adventure. We all compete for the gold medal, the blue ribbon or in this case the beautiful crown at the end of the finish line. However, if you pay attention while on the road to success you'll discover things about yourself, your universe and your God you never knew to be true.

Don't get me wrong, I still like winning; there's no feeling that compares to living that surreal moment when everything you have worked for comes together and you realize that *you did it*! And it absolutely takes ambition, drive and self-determination to make winning a possibility. But when ambition turns into obsession the unintended consequence can become very counterproductive. You inadvertently risk shifting your focus from doing what needs to be done, to a preoccupation with the end result; taking on an aura of desperation.

Most often when a "rookie competitor" came out of nowhere and stunned the audience and staff by placing or even winning the pageant it was usually because she was genuinely having a good time! If you take nothing else from reading this chapter, know that joy and enthusiasm are infectious. Know that judges are human and can't help but be drawn to a competitor with a light-hearted spirit, who is clearly *enjoying the journey.*

Enjoy The Journey

The Take Away

- Seek joy in everything you do.
- Make a conscious effort every day to take note of what you are gaining from living your specific competition experience.
- Temper your competitive intensity with a happy demeanor.
- Keep in mind that the most beautiful quality in a pageant contestant is a joyful spirit.

Debbie Barnhill – Mrs. Colorado 1993

Chapter Ten

Dreaming Is Easy – Dreams Are Not

"Courage does not always roar. Sometimes it's a quiet voice at the end of the day saying...I will try again tomorrow."
~ Mary Anne Radmacher – Writer and Artist

Have you ever noticed that children have the ability to dream really big? It's cute when they publicly declare their intentions of becoming a major league baseball player, an astronaut, the president of the United States or a famous movie star. But once we grow up we tend to lower the bar of expectations on our dreams. Some say that it's society's fault—that somehow *society* is responsible for beating us down, but I don't buy into that blame-game mentality. What I think happens is that as we grow up we encounter setbacks; maybe it's a bad test score or a disappointing loss. We mature and a part of that process causes us to think with a more realistic view of our world.

In 1982 after losing a heartbreaking struggle to conceive a biological child, I wanted to write a book on the emotional pain of infertility because back then there weren't a lot of resources on the subject. I contemplated it for quite sometime and a couple of years later as I was meandering through a book store, there on a top shelf, was "my" book; a book written about the emotional pain of infertility. *What-da-ya-know*, someone else had written "my" book.

About ten years later I got the inspired idea of writing a "Book of Letters." Letter writing can sometimes be daunting and often times it's hard to figure out where to begin. The premise of the book was to offer the reader templates of letters including thank you notes, resume cover letters, letters to doctors and lawyers, and maybe even how to begin a heartfelt love letter. I, of course, thought it was ingenious. However, the brilliant idea never got past the thought process and a couple of years later I found myself in another bookstore—and that's right—there was "my" book of letters. Yet again someone else had written a book that I had only dreamed of writing.

Years into being the pageant director I told my husband that some day I'd like to write a book about the women I had met and the funny, sometimes emotional experiences I had encountered along the way. Soon thereafter he went out and bought me a journal and suggested that I start jotting down my stories while they were still fresh memories. I'm sorry to say that I never even made *one* entry in that black leather bound journal.

In 2002 I became very sick and my family collectively thought that it would be a good idea for me to relinquish my position as the Colorado State Director and sell the very business I had spent years building. As I tried to imagine what my future would look like, I turned to my husband one night and said, "I'm too young to retire—what will I do with my days—what will I do with my life?"

And he suggested, "Why don't you write that book you've always talked about."

Hmmm, something to consider, but as it turned out I decided not to retire, I continued to work during a long and difficult recovery. But in January of 2008 I got that tap on the shoulder and once again, I heard that *still small voice* telling me that it was in fact time to pass the torch. And now, I would have the time to revisit the notion of writing a book.

I finished up with the 2008 production in May and mentored my successor during the summer. I was in charge of planning the annual Mrs. America send-off party and was enjoying the freedom of a relatively unencumbered life for the first time in seventeen years. And then as one of my final acts as the executive state director I traveled to the Mrs. America Pageant in early September to support my seventeenth and last Mrs. Colorado titleholder. In short, I just stayed busy—very busy.

When I returned home from the national pageant it gradually occurred to me that the phone wasn't ringing anymore, that the house was as clean as it could get and that for the first time in many years, I had no plan— I had no deadline to meet—I had nothing to do. I sat down at the computer that afternoon and told myself, *if you don't start writing this book today, you are never going to do it!* So I started to type. It felt good, and before I knew it, I had a comprehensive outline; I was setting deadlines for myself, and had begun working with an editor.

On October 24 just two months after I had launched the writing of my manuscript, with no indications of poor health, my mother suffered a heart attack. She was petite and fit, didn't smoke or drink and actually liked eating fruits and vegetables. Not exactly a textbook case for heart disease. Thank God my mother survived and now in light of this unexpected turn of events, it seemed perfectly clear as to why I had listened to that internal nudge to retire; because now my time and energy was needed to assist my family.

Weeks later, after life had returned to some kind of normal, I tried to begin writing again, but I just couldn't do it. I was emotionally derailed. The holidays were now upon me so I decided to put the project on hold until after the first of the year—good excuse.

In the meantime, I decided to do a little remodeling/decorating before Christmas, which included a fresh coat of interior paint and the resurfacing of our hardwood floors. Just what incendiary female gene kicks in around the holidays that compels us to take up additional projects to make our houses *Home & Garden* perfect when we already have extra things to do like putting up the seasonal decorations, power-shopping, gift wrapping, attending parties, and participating in Christmas church programs, not to mention the extraordinary cooking and baking that comes with the territory? Insanity—pure insanity!

As part of my Martha Stewart *home-perfect-project* I decided to shift all of the boxes in the storage closet to the garage. I vowed that none of them were coming back into the house until I had gone through them piece by piece to determine if we really needed all of the "stuff" that had taken up space in those plastic tubs for years. Well, Thanksgiving came and went, Christmas came and went, and then New Year's Day came and went. And much to my husband's dismay the "stuff" was still taking up space in the garage. On a freezing cold Saturday afternoon in January we both decided to tackle the mass that had now taken on a life of its own.

We brought one plastic tub in at a time and began to sift through the contents. Generally speaking, most of the things that we had saved made sense, while the contents of other boxes made no sense whatsoever. One such box was filled with scraps of upholstery fabric, my husband's golf trophies, and some random childhood memorabilia; more than likely stuff that our mothers got sick of storing and finally off-loaded it while purging their *own* storage closets. In that particular tub I found a large envelope that was given to me after my little Russian grandmother had passed away in 1997. The envelope was filled with letters I had written to her as a child. On each of the letters my grandmother had documented the month and year she received them.

As I sat cross-legged on the floor I couldn't help but take a few minutes to admire my elementary penmanship and read a couple of the letters out loud. I came across one that I had sent in 1967, making me ten years old, the first one written in cursive. It begins like this, misspelled words and all:

Dear Grandma,

How are you feeling? I hope just fine. I am wrighting a book. The name of it is "The Gost House on Wicked Hill." When I am finished with it I will send a copy to you.

I just sat there and stared at my little letter and realized that I had been talking about writing a book since I was at least ten years old. In that envelope of yellowed letters written on scrap paper and Big Chief tablets I had unearthed a buried dream—a dream that I had been carrying around for a lifetime. I guess dreaming was the easy part, but actually seeing my dream to fruition had obviously proven much more difficult. Well, that was the divine memo I needed. The very next week I was back to the computer and writing.

I've always derived inspiration from those who triumphed over obstacles *and* time; people like John Elway, Dan Jansen, along with the aforementioned Susan Lucci.

In Denver, football fans spent years banking on a quarterback by the name of John Elway to deliver a long awaited Super Bowl trophy to a team that had *never* experienced the *big* win in franchise history. Elway was drafted number one overall in the 1983 NFL Draft by the Baltimore Colts before being traded to the Denver Broncos.

By his second year in the league, he set team records for passing attempts, completions and yards, and in 1987 he led the team to Super Bowl XXI. The team didn't win and would go on to compete in two more Super Bowl games, both of which they lost, before entering a long period of serious decline.

Fans hadn't lost faith that John Elway could lead the team to a Super Bowl victory, but let's just say that he was definitely in the two minute warning of his career. Purely from a bystander's point of view, Elway's frustration was palpable; however, that would end during the 1997 season (fifteen years into his career), as Elway and Denver won their first Super Bowl title by defeating the Green Bay Packers, 31-24, in Super Bowl XXXII.

After fifteen long years, it would have been easy to become discouraged. It would have been easy to try and finagle a trade to a more promising team. It would have been easy to retire as a rich man and forget about that Super Bowl ring. But Elway didn't give up and in turn, he was not only able to make good on a personal goal, but was able to deliver a dream to his teammates, the Denver fans, and to the state of Colorado.

When I would encounter a discouraged competitor who was questioning whether or not she should return for another year, I would almost always ask her if she thought that John Elway should have given up on trying to win the Super Bowl? They rarely answered the question—they just smiled.

B.C. Forbes, founder of Forbes magazine and Editor-in-Chief until his death in 1954, once said, "History has demonstrated that the most notable winners usually encountered *heartbreaking* obstacles before they triumphed. They won because they refused to become discouraged by their defeats." You've heard the expression from *rags-to-riches?* Well, Dan Jansen's story went from *famous-for-falling* to *vindicated-by-victory.* And it all played out on the world stage; namely, the Winter Olympics.

Dan Jansen began skating when he was seven and made it to his first Winter Olympic competition as a speed skater when he was a mere eighteen years old. In his autobiography, *Full Circle* he recounts that the '84 Games in Sarajevo were probably his only "pure Olympics." He went there with pretty low expectations since not too many people knew the name of Dan Jansen. He just wanted to compete as well as he could and if he got a medal, fine; if he didn't that was okay, too.

That year he placed fourth in the 500 meters and sixteenth in the 1000 meters. Four years later he was the odds on favorite to win at least one gold medal in the 1988 Winter Olympics having become World Sprint Champion just one week before the games. However, the morning of the race, he received a phone call from home saying that his beloved sister, Jane, was losing her battle with leukemia. Jansen spoke to his unresponsive sister and later that day he was informed that she had passed.

Can you imagine? He had been preparing for this race for over fifteen years of his young life and the very day—*the very day*—of his first and best event, his sister passes away. What are the odds?

Emotionally conflicted he courageously competed that night in the 500 meters, but fell early in the race. A few days later a more composed, Jansen, competed in the 1000 meter race and began with record-breaking speed, but much to the horror of all who watched, he fell again. Dan Jansen left the 1988 Olympics with *no* medals. He was, however, awarded the U.S. Olympic Spirit Award for his valiant efforts through tragedy.

Adding insult to injury, when he returned home, according to his autobiography, there were actually people who had the audacity to poke fun of his performance.

There was a radio station that had a running joke about the towns around Milwaukee named Falls, such as Black River Falls and Menomonee Falls—perhaps West Allis should change its name to Jansen Falls, went the joke.

And then one night he and several of his friends entered the door of a restaurant, and a woman looked up and said, "Don't trip now." It's probably fair to say that no matter how noble or courageous your actions are there will always be some small-minded person poised to dismiss you on any given day.

Jansen returned to the Olympics in Albertville in 1992 again as a favorite to medal. Just the previous year he had set a world record in the 500 meters, but unexplainably misfortune struck again—he finished fourth in the 500 meters and twenty-sixth in the 1000 meters. Once again Jansen left the Olympics without a medal.

He knew what his critics were saying after Albertville: that he was a choker. His two falls in Calgary could be explained by the death of his sister, but there was no explanation for the repeat performance, when he seemed to be an absolute lock for a medal.

By now I'm not sure that I would have had the intestinal fortitude to continue, but fortunately (if you can say that there is any *fortune* associated with this story), because of format scheduling changes to the Olympics, the Winter Games in Lillehammer were only two years away instead of the standard four.

In 1994, Jansen won his second World Sprint Championships title making him the best 500 meter skater in the world! Now the 1994 Winter Olympics were Jansen's final attempt to win that elusive Olympic medal of any kind.

On February 14, 1994 exactly six years to the day his sister Jane died, he raced in his best event—the 500 meters. He slipped and finished the race in eighth place. But four days later in his *last* race in his *last* Olympic competition, a determined Dan Jansen unexpectedly won the gold medal in the race that he was least likely to win—the 1000 meters and as the national anthem played and the American flag rose, Dan Jansen stood proudly with his gold medal, looked heavenward and saluted, "This is for you, Jane. I love you."

The world of pageantry be it all a bit smaller than the NFL and the Olympics, has had its share of time-tested, or maybe better stated, time-challenged winners who persevered to win.

At the 2009 nationally televised Miss USA Pageant the outgoing titleholder had all of fifty-four seconds for her final walk. I've always found it a bit limited on the part of the Miss Universe organization to give their reigning titleholders such a miniscule amount of time to sum up their year long experience as Miss USA and express gratitude to all who shared in their successes. But I get it—it's television and things need to move along quickly, lest you lose your audience to the remote control.

Crystle Stewart, Miss USA 2008, began her final walk with these words:

After numerous losses competing for Miss Texas USA my mother said, 'The race does not go to the swift, but to the one who endures.' My dream finally became a reality affording me the opportunity to travel around the world and meet unforgettable people.

First of all I found it incredibly gracious that she would spend even one sentence of her fifty-four seconds to encourage others. I also thought it was a little unconventional, within the industry, to acknowledge past defeats given that the world of pageantry is shrouded in the mythology of perfection. Cheers to Crystle Stewart for being a *real* role model for women contemplating competition of any kind.

Crystle Stewart first competed for the Miss Texas USA title as Miss Fort Bend County where she made the semi-finals. The following year she competed again in the state pageant and placed third runner-up. In 2005 she competed for the local title of Miss Houston and placed first runner-up to Lauren Lanning, but went on to compete at the Miss Texas USA pageant as Miss Harris County and placed first runner-up to Lanning for the second time. In 2006 she placed first runner-up to Miss Houston for a second time and, in a double repetition, placed first runner-up to Miss Houston, Magen Ellis, at the state competition.

In 2007 she decided not to compete for a local title, and instead entered as an at large candidate for Miss Texas USA 2008. She made the final two in the state-televised pageant, alongside Miss Houston, Brooke Daniels, who was also a runner-up the year before, but this time Stewart won the title and was crowned Miss Texas USA 2008.

So let's recap: It took her five years, countless local titles and placing first runner-up at the state pageant two years in a row before she captured the state crown. I have to believe that her experience and her losses truly prepared her to compete for the national title and on April 11, 2008 Crystle Stewart represented Texas in the Miss USA national pageant where she became the ninth Texan to win the Miss USA title.

In the spring of 2009 I was invited to judge the Mrs. Nebraska Pageant—during the final phase of competition one of the top-five finalists was asked, "What does success mean to you?" A fairly common question asked of pageant competitors, but she gave a most uncommon answer. She replied, "Well to me success is really determined by your ability to manage your disappointments." She went on to explain that she had competed the year before and fell short of her goal—she didn't want to let the disappointment of not winning keep her from trying again. That night, Jennifer Hart, first runner-up in 2008, was crowned Mrs. Nebraska 2009.

I have an affinity for diehards. I am one. I understand the pain and the euphoria that goes along with being a person who doesn't give up. That's why people like Susan Lucci, John Elway, Dan Jansen and Crystle Stewart absolutely fascinate me. I believe that's why their lives, their stories, their trials and triumphs become a part of *our* personal narrative; we somehow compete along side of them. When they win, we win and in the process they reinforce our faith in perseverance and possibilities!

Dreaming Is Easy - Dreams Are Not

The Take Away

- Don't be afraid to dream big.
- Don't bury your dream under mounds of excuses.
- Push through procrastination, it's your enemy!
- Keep your inner self aware of your intended destination by affirming your goals, writing them down, and vocalizing them out loud every day.
- As long as it's a desire of your heart—*never* give up on a dream.

Megan Yarberry – Mrs. Colorado 2009

Chapter Eleven

Commit To Prepare — Prepare To Win

"It's not the will to win, but the will to prepare to win that makes the difference."

~ Bear Bryant – College Football Coach

The desire to win begins with the commitment to prepare. I was asked, upon more than one occasion, to describe the "perfect" title-holder. Without exception the first qualification on my wish list was a person who was not only committed, but also ambitious.

During the last year of my directorship a contestant walked into my office, looked at the headshots of the Mrs. Colorado titleholders on the wall above my desk and asked, "What *one* quality do they all possess—what makes them similar?" What a great question and one that I had to consider before answering. At first glance the differences were more apparent than the similarities. Of the seventeen representatives I've intimately worked with, their profiles ranged from a forty-year-old, well-educated nurse anesthetist to a twenty-three-year-old make-up artist with a high school diploma. Some were short, some were tall, some were exotic looking while others resembled the wholesome girl next door and many of them came from very different socio-economic backgrounds. So what was it that made these women similar?

After giving it some thought I came to the conclusion that the one thing they all had in common was a competitive spirit and that they were all very committed to preparing for the competition. In short, they were coachable learners.

Somewhere along the way I understood that my mission as the director to the Mrs. Colorado Pageant was to "guide and direct." In fact about six years ago I actually developed an official mission statement for the pageant:

"The mission of the Mrs. Colorado Pageant is to inspire women to seek personal excellence through preparation and competition."

Notice that the statement includes the word "preparation." I also authored a personal mission statement that was written directly under the daily to-do list on my computer that read:

"As the director it is my mission to provide Purpose, Direction and Motivation, to help women accomplish their goals through competition."

I felt it was my obligation to provide the contestants who crossed the threshold of my pageant system with knowledge of the process so that each individual could prepare for success. However, it was *their* obligation to commit to prepare.

Every year there was at least one contestant who signed up for the pageant a year in advance and then showed up to my office on the day of the final deadline, with her paperwork and photograph in hand. Once a contestant actually rang my doorbell at midnight to turn in her required materials! Finally, I not only had to put a date on the deadline, but an actual time limit as well. These people procrastinated what seemed like the most minor details until the last possible minute—in essence there was no real commitment to prepare.

At the same time I was always pleasantly surprised by the contestant who would sign up weeks before the competition and proficiently accomplish the very same tasks in a matter of days. You see committing to prepare has nothing to do with time, it has everything to do with drive and motivation. Commitment has to take place in the heart as well as the mind.

Obviously, preparing for pageantry as well as any other competition or sport takes a fair amount of dedication and organization. Each leg of the competition should be approached with equal commitment and enthusiasm. And while it was not my intention to write a "how-to book," I still thought it was necessary to address the fundamental elements of pageant competition and the basics on how to begin.

How And Where To Start

There's an old Broadway tune that goes like this: "A song is not a song until you sing it, a bell is not a bell until you ring it." Well a dream is only a dream until the abstract thought transcends into physical action. After all, you can't win the lottery unless you buy a ticket. In order to become a contestant for America's newest sensation on the latest reality show, you must first go through the audition process. And the first steps to achieving a degree are to apply to a university and take the entrance exam.

So, before making the commitment to enter any competition do your research. In the case of pageantry, study the website, if one exists, and if possible, purchase a video or DVD of last year's production and a program book. Speak directly to the pageant's executive director and discuss any questions or concerns you may have prior to making a financial deposit. This should give you ample information on how the pageant operates and if it's a good match for you.

Once you've made the mental commitment then take the first step to entering and get organized, more than likely you'll begin to receive paperwork from the state or national director. In order to keep track of all communiqués, forms and mailings, create a system that works for you; perhaps a binder or a small file box where you can easily store and access information. Being structured should also keep you on target with deadlines and goals.

Paperwork

I always suggest typing your paperwork. Treat every form that you turn into the director as if it's your college thesis or final exam. Most pageant systems now make their forms available online, which makes the process much easier. Absolutely never handwrite any form that will be viewed by the judges. Even if you have great penmanship, it's always much harder for a judge to navigate handwritten materials; not to mention they appear unprofessional.

Most pageant systems will ask you to submit some sort of a biography form. This gives the judges a brief profile on your personal history. I've judged pageants where I was asked to review the biographies weeks in advance of the competition and then I've judged pageants where I was given all of the biographies just hours before competition for a brief review. Either way the biography form sets the intellectual and emotional tone of your interview.

It should be well written, sans any misspelled words or typos. It should be comprehensive and to the point; highlighting things you wish for them to know about you. Don't make the mistake of writing too much. It's not an assignment in novel writing, and more is not better in this case. Keep your information in the parameters of the form provided. Never extend your margins and don't bother attaching an additional paper to the biography; nine times out of ten a judge won't see it, or won't have the time to actually read it.

And finally before returning your paperwork, be sure to make copies for future study and reference. Again, being organized can help relieve any undue pressure as competition time draws near.

Raising Sponsorships

Most, if not all participants in competitive activities, will seek sponsors to defray the costs associated with competing. Think about it—cyclists, NASCAR racers, gymnasts, Little League Baseball teams, bowling leagues, skiers and snowboarders all have sponsors who make competing in their given activities possible. Unless you are one of a very small group of independently wealthy people, then raising the money to participate is just part of the game. It wasn't necessarily one of my favorite things to do as a contestant or a director (yes directors spend a lot of time finding sponsors who will provide the prize packages for both the winner and the delegates), however, once I got started it really wasn't that painful and I found that the more people I approached the more people said yes. At some level, it's just a numbers game, but you have to be willing to extend yourself.

By obtaining outside sponsors, you should be able to enter a pageant at little or no cost to you or your family. Here are the techniques success-fully used by thousands of pageant contestants.

First and foremost, get an early start. Share the good news about your intentions with your family, friends and community. Make certain they understand the exceptional opportunity provided if you should win and advance to compete nationally, and how that translates into publicity opportunities for them as well.

Locating willing sponsors can be as easy as looking in the register of your checkbook. Who have you supported or patronized within the past six months—grocer, doctor, dentist, insurance agent, clothing store, dry cleaner, restaurant, gas station, beauty salon, specialty stores? And don't rule out that often an employer can also be a potential candidate for sponsorship.

Don't be afraid to ask extended family, friends and neighbors to be sponsors. Some contestants have been sponsored by their parents, aunts, uncles, cousins and grandparents. They will respond, but you need to make the request. And don't ask one sponsor to cover all of your expenses; you will have greater success asking for a reasonable sum from many individuals.

Try to meet potential sponsors in person. It helps to dress professionally and have a letter you can give them detailing the competition you have entered and your personal goals. A sponsor is more likely to say yes if you ask in person. Never present yourself as a charitable cause, but rather as a community representative who is soliciting local support. Most importantly, don't get discouraged if you run into disappointments at the beginning. Keep trying. For every person who says no, there will be many who will say yes, and before you know it you will have successfully raised your funds.

Selecting A Good Photographer And Headshot

A good headshot is invaluable in pageant competition for several reasons. It's really your first opportunity to impress the judges since in most pageants they receive the program book in advance of meeting you. Second, and more importantly, judges will use the program book to take notes and almost always refer back to photographs when making their final selections during preliminary rounds of competition.

First, find a photographer who specializes in headshot photography. Your best source for recommendations is your state director. If he or she has no suggestions then call your local talent/modeling agency as they usually have the region's "A list" of photographers.

Ask to look at samples of their work before committing to a photo shoot and make sure you get a price list, not only for the shoot, but for prints and enlargements.

Never sign a model's release form unless you are willing to let them use your image in any conceivable way. If a photographer is sponsoring your photo shoot then you will probably be required to sign a release.

I highly recommend hiring a professional make-up artist to do your make-up, and I don't mean the neighborhood woman who sells products from home. Camera make-up is completely different from every day make-up. It requires contouring and subtle shading and a skilled artist will know what colors work best with your skin tone and lighting. The right make-up can mean the difference between an acceptable photo and an amazing photo.

If you have a lot of weight to lose, or you plan to change your hair color or style, then wait until you have achieved your desired look before having your headshot taken.

Wear simple necklines, solid colors, minimal jewelry and no hats. The idea is to feature *you,* not your sense of fashion. Do not select a photo where your hands are touching your face or hair. That too can prove to be more of a distraction.

Select a headshot that's glamorous (not to be confused with Glamour Shots), but also approachable, warm and friendly. Going for the *runway-model-I've-got-attitude* look wouldn't be my first choice.

Finally and most importantly, the photo should look like you! Retouching is fine, but I've seen photographers go overboard. Getting rid of a temporary blemish or *some* fine lines is acceptable, but do *not* alter your features. Here's a good rule of thumb: If a friend looks at your picture and says, "Is that *you*?" It's not a good sign.

Upon more than one occasion after interview competition a judge would call me over to his or her desk, point to the program book and ask, "Who is this?" In every case, the photo didn't look like the contestant. *Mmm… yeah*, not a good sign.

The Interview Competition

Because "beauty queens" are usually, if not always, ambassadors for a program or spokesmodels for a brand, they are expected to attend social functions and are quite often asked to address the public; sometimes without any prior notice. Not only is she required to speak at charitable events and high profile fundraisers, but she also needs to be comfortable visiting with patients at hospitals, children in schools, and residents in long-term care facilities. Ideally, she needs to be able to communicate the importance of others.

To the outsider, the position of pageant titleholder/beauty queen may seem like a self-centered endeavor, but it truly is a position of service. Thus, communication skills are vitally important.

Ralph Waldo Emerson once said, "Beauty without expression is boring." And that's precisely why the personal interview is, in my opinion, the most important phase of pageant competition. However, it was my experience as the director that it was also the most neglected or ignored category of competition when it came to preparation. I saw contestants that had dieted and exercised all year until they looked like swimsuit models and then about two weeks prior to the competition would call and ask if I had any suggestions on how to prepare for the personal interview. Right about then my mind would begin to spin with thoughts like— *you mean you're just now getting around to thinking about the interview competition?*

Each year I would study the scores after the pageant was over and every year the winner would come out of the personal interview placing in the top five. She didn't always win the "Best in Interview" award, but she came out of the preliminary round of interview competition as one of the top five finishers. This was true for seventeen consecutive years— arguably that's a pretty powerful statistic!

Now that the importance of personal interview has been established, it's necessary that you make an individual assessment. Do you consider yourself to be an effective communicator, especially under pressure? Reflect back on job interviews and past performances. Once you've done that then put together a strategy that will work for your particular needs.

Unlike the physical fitness competition where resources for preparation are unlimited, preparing for personal interview can be somewhat confusing and contestants many times find themselves at a loss as to where to begin. So where *does* one start?

Here is a list of possible suggestions ranging from simple, inexpensive exercises to a more elaborate plan to work with a professional coach.

- The easiest thing you can do is to purchase a book on the topic of interview techniques. Many good books have been written on the subject and can usually be found in the business section of your local library or bookstore.

- Make copies of your personal biography and give them to five of your closest friends or family members. Ask each of them to call you once a week and ask you a question directly from the form. You'll be amazed at how each individual will find different ways to ask the same question. It's a simple exercise to keep your mind limber.

- You can purchase a list of questions to help you work on content. The intention is not to create and memorize answers, but rather to assist you in organizing your thoughts and concepts. It's an exercise designed to shore up your self-confidence in answering off-the-cuff questions.

- Ask someone you know and respect to give you a mock interview and video record the session. This proved to be a great exercise, especially for visual learners.

- If you really struggle with communication then I would suggest hiring a professional coach, but one who specializes in personal interview techniques. The most effective coaches work with individuals in person, not long distance over the telephone. It's impossible to coach someone with regards to eye contact and body language without physically seeing them.

I loved training women in interview as it was always my strongest category in competition. Besides giving my own contestants a complimentary one hour session, for many years, I also trained girls/women who competed in other pageant systems. Here are a few tips to remember when working on personal interview.

- Assume a comfortable, but professional posture. I've never believed that sitting on the edge of your chair, with your ankles and hands crossed looked very approachable.
- Maintain good eye contact. Countless times I witnessed women who, when asked a question, instinctively looked up to the ceiling then down to the floor as if they were searching for an answer. It doesn't bode well for self-confidence.
- Don't rush to speak. It's better to take a couple of seconds to respond to a question than to start talking in circles before you get to the point, just so you can fill a moment of what seems like uncomfortable silence.
- You're body language should be relaxed and expressive. It's okay to talk with your hands, that's only natural, however, don't point or get carried away with grand gestures.
- Speak with confidence and authority. Many women I worked with actually had good content in their answers, but spoke with trepidation. Whatever you say, say it with conviction!
- Your answers should be succinct. If you find yourself repeating the theme of your answer then it's time to wrap it up, make your point and move on.
- Illustrate your point with a story or anecdote rather than spewing philosophy. Anytime you can deliver an answer that directly relates to a personal experience I guarantee you will be perceived as more compelling and ultimately more memorable.
- Always be honest, but diplomatic. Disingenuous never works.

- Prepare, but don't become rehearsed. The term "Pageant Patty" is most often used in reference to the contestant who has every answer rehearsed and delivers it like an automaton showing very little of her own personality and charm.
- If for some reason you are asked a question that strikes a personal cord, it's completely acceptable to express emotion; speaking with emotional power can be very effective. But it's not okay to become unhinged—stay in control of your emotions.

The Swimsuit/Physical Fitness Competition

The swimsuit competition can easily be broken down into two parts; physical fitness and physical self-confidence. Each is *equally* important! You can have a great body and a terrible walk and be overlooked, or have a great walk and a terrible physique and be discounted.

Part One – Physical Fitness

Physical fitness obviously encompasses weight management and muscle tone. The best way to achieve your goals in a healthy responsible manner is to get an early start. For women who had serious weight issues, usually people who had more than twenty pounds to lose, I suggested that they join a support program like Weight Watchers or Jenny Craig. It's also very valuable to solicit the help of a personal trainer, however, that is usually pretty costly. At the very minimum it would be a good idea to hire a personal trainer to create a workout that addresses your specific challenges.

Another easy and affordable way to stay accountable to weight loss is to join forces with a friend who would also like to get in shape. The "buddy system" really works for women because we're social creatures. Weight loss is a challenging commitment and most often we are successful when we can make it fun.

If you're like me and find the gym to be an uninspiring place then finding an activity you enjoy rather than a dry workout is paramount to success. Join a Salsa dance class, take brisk early morning walks with a neighbor, or if you're a mom, spend an hour every evening shooting baskets on the driveway with your kids. In other words, find ways to make exercise entertaining and personally fulfilling.

Ultimately be mindful that in order to achieve true success you must be willing to exercise daily and make healthy diet choices. It's that combination that provides the best results.

Part Two – Physical Self-Confidence

Most often it was the competitor new to pageantry that would struggle with appearing natural or self-confident on stage and it always dramatically affected their scores. Physical self-confidence can be achieved with practice, but first you need to make a shoe selection that's appropriate for your skill level. I would rather see a short woman with an incredible walk than a woman who appears tall with an awkward walk because she's wearing five inch heels. Select a heel height that best suits your abilities and comfort level. Purchase your competition shoes as soon as possible and three to five times a week put them on and walk to music on a hard surface for at least fifteen minutes. Make sure your shoulders are rolled back and your posture is erect, lifting from your diaphragm. You should appear confident, but relaxed.

Practice smiling a natural warm expression rather than a plastered stiff grin. My dance instructor used to insist in every class that her students not only dance, but also rehearse performing with their facial expressions. At first you may feel silly, but sometimes the action needs to precede the feeling. After awhile you'll get used to the familiar, comfortable feeling of smiling while performing. Use a mirror or even a video camera to help you identify any potential problems.

If you are having difficulty on your own, dance classes always helped people who struggled with posture. You can burn calories and foster good posture all in the same exercise and it's a very affordable option.

If you still feel as though you are missing the mark, then I highly recommend a couple of private lessons with a modeling coach in addition to lots of practice. In the end it will prove to be an all around valuable investment.

Plastic Surgery

In case I wasn't perfectly clear in chapter five, "Be Fearless – Not Reckless," let me say it one more time. Bust lines don't win pageants. Skilled competitors do. Having said that, if there's something that you wish to change about your appearance I don't have an ethical or moral problem with plastic surgery, but the motivation for the surgery should *not* be to win a pageant.

Also, I would never advise plastic surgery for cosmetic purposes to any person under the age of eighteen. (Obviously with the exception of correcting a congenital deformity or an accident related injury.) It's a major decision and should only be considered upon adulthood, once a person has reached physical and emotional maturity.

Because of my unique career choice I was often asked for my opinion about plastic surgery and recommendations for plastic surgeons, not only from competitors, but from friends and acquaintances alike. However, even though I worked in an image-based industry, it by no means made me an expert on either topic—but this is what I *did* learn over the course of seventeen years.

First and foremost make sure that the doctor you select is a board certified plastic surgeon. I would advise you to shop for a doctor even though you will more than likely pay for each consultation. In the long run it's a small price to pay in order to find the right surgeon. I would suggest at least three opinions before making a final decision.

Be proactive. Make a list of questions about the procedure you are seeking and make sure you've adequately communicated your desired results.

Never let the doctor/surgeon make key decisions about "your look." I knew two women who relinquished total autonomy to doctors who had bullied them with the line, "I'm the doctor—I know what's best." In both situations the women ended up with disastrous results. One came out with a nose too small for her face and the other ended up with breasts too big for her body. Just because there's an M.D. behind their names doesn't give them the right to make your personal decisions.

And most importantly remember that plastic surgery *permanently* alters your body.

The Evening Gown Competition

The words evening gown and pageantry are synonymous; like Cinderella and glass slipper, like bride and wedding dress, like movie star and sunglasses.

The gown is undoubtedly the most important clothing purchase you'll make. After all, you don't get crowned in your interview outfit or swimsuit. In the last phases of pageant competition the contestant always advances in her evening gown. Having said that, I don't think a *spectacular* gown wins a pageant, but I do think the *wrong* gown can keep a good competitor from winning. Once the field of competition has been narrowed to top five, the judges are left to decide between five very strong candidates who up until this point have done enough right to be in the final circle for consideration. If a judge ends up being torn between two finalists, a great gown and how she wears it or a great final answer are the last determining factors. So here is some basic advice when looking for that *perfect* dress.

I'm not one who believes that the price tag determines the value of the evening gown, but I do think that fit, color, and how it plays on a stage are important factors to consider when choosing a competition dress.

It should fit like it was made for your body and length is important since the stage is usually elevated. Many gowns in department stores are made for social occasions and not for pageant competition. They are usually ankle length or a couple of inches off of the floor when wearing heels. From the judge's angle (which is usually lower than the stage), this can look like an exaggerated four inches; so make sure that your gown just brushes above the top of your shoe.

Choose a color that doesn't wash out under the intensity of stage lighting; for example baby blue can sometimes turn grey and pastel pink can end up looking like a flesh tone. Usually earth tones do not appear glamorous without a lot of beading or embellishment. White, black, and jewel tones usually do very well in various venues and different lighting.

The gown should reflect your personal style, but should also have qualities that make it stand out on stage; every detail takes on a unique importance like beading, high quality crystals and movement of fabric. More is not necessarily best, but the gown does need to capture the eye.

Style and trends change and pageantry is no exception to that rule. Purchasing a second-hand gown is acceptable, but I wouldn't recommend buying anything that is over two years old. If you do, you definitely run the risk of looking outdated.

Most of all, wearing a gown is about feeling beautiful. It's about gracing the stage with glamour, style and personality. In short, your gown should make you feel invincibly magical.

The Talent Competition

I directed a pageant that didn't happen to include performing talent as a requirement, but I felt it was important to address the topic for my readers who may be contemplating entering such a competition. So I contacted the national Miss America organization and requested an interview.

Most Americans still consider the Miss America Pageant as the gold standard in the industry and for good reason—most notably because it was the first. The Miss America competition originated on September 8, 1921, as a two-day beauty contest in Atlantic City, New Jersey. The pageant was initiated in an attempt to keep tourists in Atlantic City after the Labor Day weekend. Performing talent wasn't added to the competition until 1935.

Today, the Miss America scholarship program, along with its local and state affiliates, is the largest provider of scholarship money to young women in the world, and in 2006 made available more than $45 million in cash and scholarship assistance.

During the preliminary competitions, the performing talent counts for thirty-five percent of a contestant's overall score and during the finals competition, performing talent counts for thirty percent of a competitor's final score. This scoring system remains exactly the same during local, state, and national competitions, so, obviously performing talent is heavily weighted in this program. My list of questions directed to the marketing director, Bonnie MacIsaac, included the question, "Should young women who are considering entering this competition work with a talent coach?"

This was her reply: "We do not make these sorts of recommendations. Each contestant is different and it is up to her and her director whether or not they would like to work with a talent coach."

While that was a noncommittal answer, and vague at best, I understand that it was probably difficult to make a recommendation in the macro. I think it's fair to say that if talent counts for such a large portion of your score that this would probably be the *one* category where it would be imperative to solicit the direction of a coach. It only makes sense. A coach who is specifically trained in your discipline is truly the only qualified person to give you guidance.

Also, your physical presentation in talent is a big part of the visual aspect of your performance. Your costume, hair and make-up should fit the overall vision and expression of your performing talent.

Preparing For The Final Question

I once had a contestant ask, "What's the difference between a question and a top five question?" At face value her question was a bit silly. A question is a question. The difference isn't about the question it's about the delivery of the answer. When you're questioned in personal interview you are communicating in an intimate setting; sometimes with one judge and at most a small panel of judges. In that setting you are not only being scored on the content of your answer, but your interpersonal communication skills as well.

In the top five round of questioning you are, in effect, addressing an entire audience. You are not only being judged on the content of your answer, but on the style in which you deliver it. Your public speaking ability is what's truly being judged.

The top five question is "high stakes" as it can be a make-or-break moment in a competitor's experience. Composure, body language, a succinct delivery and the use of the microphone are all strategic components that comprise a winning performance. But there's also something else to consider when answering a question in a public format, and that's your personal value system.

There's a scene in the movie *Miss Congeniality* where the top five finalists are asked to answer a question which is pretty standard fare for a pageant. All of the finalists make sure that their answer includes the words "world peace." That is, all but the pageant rookie who is really the FBI plant played by Sandra Bullock. She begins to deliver a heartfelt, realistic response until she senses an uncomfortable silence come over the audience and it dawns on her that she *too* needs to say "world peace."

It's an old joke for sure, but do you want to know why that ridiculous "bimbo stereotype" has stuck to pageantry and pageant titleholders? It's because there is *nothing* controversial or politically incorrect about wishing for "world peace." *Seriously*—who doesn't wish for the world to live in peace? It really doesn't take a deep thinker to come up with that answer.

It was my experience as both a director and a judge that pageant contestants were more than capable of analytical thinking, but most often defaulted for the "safe" answer.

While writing this book, the controversy between Miss California, Carrie Prejean and the Miss USA Pageant erupted when Prejean was asked a question that required her to express an opinion about gay marriage in America.

When she began speaking I thought—*well she's going with the "safe" answer, one that requires very little courage or authenticity.* But midway through her answer she changed direction and decided to honestly state her opinion. And for that, judge number eight not only penalized her, but went on to publicly blast her on his entertainment blog. Literally overnight, Carrie Prejean became a household name.

First of all, I don't think the question belonged in a pageant competition. I think that the Miss Universe organization should have vetted the judge's questions in advance of the live telecast. These are young women in their early twenties, not seasoned politicians. During the 2008 national election, then Senator Obama, a forty-seven-year-old, Harvard graduate, reluctantly answered a question about the "definition of marriage." He knew it was a loaded question and not coincidentally his opinion didn't differ much from that of Miss California's.

The controversy grew daily and eventually ended with the character assassination of Prejean before ultimately being stripped of her Miss California USA title and crown. Litigation followed and a settlement was eventually reached. In effect we've done to beauty queens what we've done to our politicians. If they tell us the truth we won't vote for them. If they side-step an answer by sitting on the proverbial fence then they've rendered themselves as ineffective communicators whom we summarily dismiss because they're not believable.

I not only thought Miss California was daring *and* honest, but I also thought that she politely delivered her answer with considerable grace.

So I decided to call a couple of people who I admire in the industry to get their perspective on what they thought of Miss California's answer. I was truly surprised at some of my colleague's reactions. One of whom specializes in pageant coaching vehemently disagreed with me saying, "Listen, I coach my clients to *win* pageants; I would have advised her to stay politically correct no matter what."

Women have tolerated the "double standard" forever. I don't suspect that it will change anytime in the near future, but I'll look forward to the day when a reporter runs up to the quarterback who has just led his team to a Super Bowl victory and shoves a microphone in his face to ask him what he thinks about gay marriage, illegal immigration, or gun control. Then and only then will I consider it fair to ask a "beauty queen" the same questions.

I guess Miss California should have stuck with the time-tested answer— "world peace." In the end it is *you* who must wrestle with this decision. What are you willing to say to win a pageant and what values are you not willing to compromise to win a pageant? It's your call to make.

Developing Mental Strength And A Winning Attitude

I already discussed the power of believing that "you can" in chapter four and the value of developing a winning mental attitude. It was my faith that played a valuable role in my journey because it was prayer that gave me the courage to rise above my nerves. And I truly feel that it was my faith that allowed me to believe that I could do it. I didn't *always* win, but I *always* believed I could. And because I *always* believed I could, I never feared trying.

Part One – Developing Mental Strength Through Discipline And Focus

My husband loves to golf, so over the years I've watched many national and international golf tournaments on lazy Sunday afternoons. After awhile what I discovered about golf was that it's a lot like pageantry. Unlike boxing where you need to beat up your opponent to win, golfers just need to show up and play their personal best. You never see a golfer trash-talking another golfer over a sand trap. I think most people would agree that the game of golf more than any other sport requires intense mental discipline.

It was my experience in pageantry that the women who were guilty of playing "mind games" never won. They spent way too much emotional energy paying attention to everyone else and lost focus of their own performance.

Now I don't doubt that golfers check out the field of competition and occasionally take note of the leader board to see who's in the lead, but for the most part, their concentration has to be on their *own* game.

On August 16, 2009, the one hundred-tenth ranked player in the world, Y.E. Yang of South Korea beat the number one ranked, Tiger Woods. During an interview, Yang joked, "I know Tiger isn't going to beat me up on the green. I just play cool and easy."

An article written for *Time* magazine states that Yang also believed in his ability, saying that his success was no fluke, "Going head to head against the mighty Woods is something I sort of visualized quite a few times, playing with him in the final round of a major championship." Yang said after his unbelievable victory, "I always sort of dreamed about this."

He dreamed about it, he visualized it and ultimately he believed it was possible. Proving that on any given day the best can be beaten and the underdog can win.

Part Two – Developing A Winning Attitude

While developing mental strength has to do with believing that you can win, developing a winning attitude isn't just about winning; sometimes it's about summoning the mental and physical stamina to finish what you've started and learn from the process. As you learn from your experience you can't help, but gain the self-confidence to believe that winning is a real possibility.

On April 26, 2009, during the NASCAR Talladega 500, Carl Edwards was leading the race in the final lap when he went to block a car from passing. A second attempt to block went horribly wrong and sent his car airborne. It did a three hundred sixty degree flip, bounced off of the catch fencing and landed in a ball of flames. It was hard to imagine that Edwards was not seriously injured. However, much to the spectators' relief, as the camera panned in for a close-up, they saw him struggle to release his restraints and climb out of the driver's window. What happened next was truly remarkable. After his car was destroyed just yards from the start/finish line Carl Edwards began to run.

The commentators questioned:

"Not sure where Carl's going? Maybe he thinks if he runs across the start/finish line that it'll count."

"That's what he's doing!" Then he screamed, "*That's what he's doing!*"

"You know how he is—he's an athlete—a marathon runner—I want to finish the race—and *he did* to a standing ovation from the crowd!"

Carl Edwards was given credit for finishing in twenty-fourth place and in a television interview the next morning Edwards commented, "I was just too close not to finish."

Later in an article he was quoted, "I did learn something about the end of the race—block once, but I probably won't block twice. Really, personally, I feel good about it. I think that wreck showed me you can have a pretty wild wreck and walk away from it."

Not winning doesn't make you a loser—but being a poor-sport does! Believe that you can win—if you don't win, learn from your experience and always have the perseverance as well as the grace to finish the race!

Preparing For The Competition Experience

I began this chapter with the concept of organization and I'm going to end it with the same advice. I've often related pageant competition to a rollercoaster ride. It's really exciting, but when you're done you can feel a little woozy. Once you've accomplished everything in your power to make yourself competitive, then make sure you've left no detail to chance as you prepare for the actual competition; whether it takes place over a weekend in your hometown or over three weeks in another state or country. The preparation you do before you compete can effectively reduce your stress level, thus ensuring you of a more positive experience.

One – Make A Packing List

I actually supplied a packing list to my contestants, but in the event that you don't have one, then create a personal check list of your own. Below is a basic list of categories and under each category make a list of everything you may need:

- Interview Competition
- Opening Production Number
- Swimsuit Competition
- Evening Gown Competition
- Talent Competition
- Daily Wardrobe
- Personal Items
- Make-up
- Food and Energy Drinks

Two – Do A Wardrobe Check

Try on your entire wardrobe just days before leaving for the competition. Make sure that last minute nerves didn't cause an unintended weight loss that would necessitate altering your clothes. Check for any loose buttons.

Always pack extra accessories and necessities like underwear and bust pads just to be on the safe side.

Three – Hair And Make-up

Always do a trial run whether you are in charge of doing your own hair and make-up or you are hiring professionals. Take photos of the final result so you can refer to it at a later date.

Four – Confirm All Appointments

If you've made appointments with a make-up artist and a hair stylist, then call before you leave for the competition to confirm all dates, locations and times. Always have both a business phone contact and a personal cell phone number in case there is a miscommunication or a last minute change in scheduling.

Five – Be Willing To Negotiate And Set Boundaries With Your Roommate

In most, if not all, pageants where you are required to stay at the host hotel for the competition you will more than likely have a roommate. You usually have no control over whom you are coupled with so it's wise to communicate expectations with your roommate as soon as possible.

Getting along with your roommate can mean the difference between having a positive experience and a very trying time. It's best if you don't view your roommate as a fellow competitor, but rather as a friend. I know it sounds a bit like mental gymnastics (and it is), but you have to spend a lot of downtime in your room together. During my national experience I took my roommate a small personal gift to ensure that we got off to a friendly start and as the director I suggested to each of my titleholders that they do the same.

When I went to the national Mrs. America Pageant I was there for seventeen days. That's a long time to share space with a stranger/new friend. Early on, my roommate, Mrs. Maryland and I made a pact. We decided that the room was our sanctuary. We agreed that we would talk about the events of the day and the other competitors as a way to recap our experience, but that we would only talk about it for a maximum of fifteen minutes. After that, these specific subjects were off limits because we desperately needed to decompress. You'll go crazy if it's all you think about.

We came to a satisfactory compromise on how we would share the closet and bathroom/mirror time. Sounds elementary, but if you are always jockeying for your space it can be a real nightmare.

And finally, it's a good idea to set boundaries on your incoming calls and guests as not to disrupt your roommate's privacy and ability to get good rest. It goes without saying that common courtesy should always be the rule, not the exception.

Commit To Prepare - Prepare To Win

The Take Away

- Make the mental commitment to compete sooner rather than later.
- Research the competition you are contemplating and then enter.
- The first step in preparation is to get organized.
- Get an early start on fundraising.
- Interview preparations shouldn't be an afterthought.
- The key to a good physique is being dedicated to a lifestyle of healthy diet and exercise. No crash dieting or diet pills!

Continued

- Your evening gown should be *spectacular*. It should be form fitting, a good color choice, and the appropriate length.
- Approach the delivery of your top five answer as an exercise in public speaking.
- Developing a winning attitude is more important than plastic surgery.
- Final preparations will go smoothly if you take an organized approach.
- Be proactive and set mutually agreed upon boundaries and understandings with your pageant roommate.

Sheri Engstrom – Mrs. Colorado 2004

Chapter Twelve

Blessings Beyond The Crown

"When we lose one blessing, another is often,
most unexpectedly, given in its place."
~ C.S. Lewis – Novelist and Academic

In the introduction I made note of the fact that I never set out to become a pageant director. I acknowledged that my life had taken on a rhythm all its own that led me to this place, and I truly feel blessed that it did. I made friends with incredible women along the way and met some of the finest examples of "yes people" who sincerely had to overcome serious hurdles in order to participate.

I began this book by asking the question, "Why do women compete in pageants?" The following stories illustrate what I like to call *blessings beyond the crown*. I found it interesting that the times when someone had felt particularly moved, touched or blessed by the experience of competing, and yet not winning the crown, it also resulted in a bonus blessing for me as well.

Elfriede Flanery

I was three years into my directorship when I got a call from Elfriede Flanery. She told me that she was nearly sixty years old, but that many people thought she looked much younger than her age. I told her she met the basic qualifications and that she was welcome to join the competition. I was a relatively new director and admittedly still on the learning curve. I found it a bit curious as to why someone her age would want to compete. Needless to say I had a narrow-minded attitude about the profile of likely contestants and I still had a lot to learn.

To look at Elfriede, you wouldn't classify her as the traditional, run-of-the-mill pageant competitor. Besides her age, she was short and stout—good German stock and still had a fairly thick accent. Elfriede was a post World War II bride, who met her husband, Brian, an American soldier, while on a tour of duty in Europe.

During an afternoon break after a long morning of rehearsals I saw Elfriede sitting alone hunched over her sacked lunch crying. I thought, *Oh, for the love of Sam, someone has picked on this dear woman.* I lurched to a stop, sat down and put my arm around her. I pulled her close and asked what was wrong.

Swiping at the tears on her face, she reached into the little brown bag and retrieved a small folded piece of paper. She told me that her husband had packed her lunch that morning and had included a short note. It read: "Over the past forty years you have sacrificed everything to be my wife, now this one's for you."

Elfriede was overwhelmed with emotion. I honestly think that this may have been the first time her husband had conveyed such a sentiment. That year Elfriede won the award for "Longest Married" and when the pageant was over, Brian Flanery worked his way through the crowd headed in my direction. I assumed he was going to comment on the production or something of that nature, but instead he said, "Wasn't she beautiful—wasn't she *just* beautiful?" Pride emanated from his very being.

On the following Monday morning the doorbell rang and the delivery man stood there with the most lavish arrangement of red, white and blue flowers, which also included some small American flags. Mistakenly I assumed they were from my newly crowned titleholder, but much to my surprise they were from the Flanerys thanking me for a wonderful experience.

Two years later Elfriede called my office more than a little distraught. She told me that Brian had been diagnosed with a terminal illness and that she wanted to do the pageant one more time in honor of their marriage. I simply responded, "Let's do it!"

During evening gown competition the night of pageant finals, Elfriede walked on to stage and out of the corner of my eye I saw her frail, weak husband wearing his dress blues from so long ago, stand and give her a salute. It was truly one of the most precious moments of my career.

Not long after the 1997 pageant, Brian Flanery passed away. Elfriede asked me to be one of several people to deliver his eulogy. I accepted the invitation and when I arrived at the mortuary chapel her tiara, sash, and a photo of the two of them, taken at the pageant, adorned his casket.

The Flanerys taught me to look at this competition and its competitors with an *inclusive* attitude—that the "beauty" in "beauty pageant" meant more than being pretty. I no longer questioned a person's qualifications or motives for entering. Now I viewed my job as facilitating one shining moment in a woman's life when she was fulfilling a desire of her heart. As much as the pageant had apparently blessed them, it was truly my honor to have crossed paths with this very unique couple—the Flanerys!

Elfriede's blessing beyond the crown – Revelation...

Nancy Driller

Nancy Driller's story is truly one of serendipity—a chance encounter that was about to change her life. Nancy found herself standing in a long line at a pharmacy waiting patiently to fill yet another prescription. Having just been told by her doctor that her thirty-year-old body resembled that of a sixty-year-old she felt defeated. She silently prayed while struggling to keep her composure.

Nancy had been diagnosed as menopausal in her early twenties and was now suffering the devastating physical consequences including full-blown osteoporosis. She had long dealt with the emotional embarrassment of her condition and the reality that she would never have biological children, but now her health was deteriorating. In her own words she described that day in the pharmacy:

> *My eyes filled with tears to the point they were about to spill over. I didn't want to cry in public so I stopped praying and went about the business of writing my check and digging through my purse just to look occupied.*
>
> *I finally reached the front of the line, quickly finished up business and grabbed my prescription. By now the tears were beginning to blur my vision. I pivoted towards the door to make a quick exit when someone caught my arm. She handed me a card and mentioned something about being a "good candidate." I took the card and brushed her off.*
>
> *Inside the safety of my car with the doors locked and the windows closed I began to sob uncontrollably. Taking quick, sharp breaths that come after a good cry, I looked at the business card the stranger had given me. Blinking a few times to make sure my eyes weren't deceiving me I was holding a business card for the Mrs. Colorado Pageant that included contact information. Terri Pepe, a former contestant noticed me in the pharmacy and decided to recruit me for the competition. I sarcastically looked up and yelled at God, 'What? Now you want to pour salt in my wounds?'*

Nancy later wrote me a letter describing her journey to pageant competition and how the experience had changed her life.

I'll never know for sure what prompted me to call the number, but before I knew it I had been selected as the state representative for Douglas County. I began lifting weights to gain confidence for the swimsuit competition. Even though I didn't place that year I returned for a second time and got more serious about weight training and added more cardio exercise to my routine.

By my third and final year I was so serious about staying in shape that when I went in for my yearly physical and bone density test I was informed that I had actually gained bone mass and had even regained a quarter of an inch in height. The doctor had made the decision to dramatically reduce my medications; the very ones I had stood in line for three years earlier.

I believe that God used the pageant to restore my health and build my self-confidence at one of the lowest points in my life. I now shutter to think of how I may have dealt with the feelings of hopelessness.

A couple of years later Nancy and I spoke about her experience and she told me that besides the overall improvement in her health, the increased self-esteem she garnered from competing translated into a new level of respect at work and eventually led to several job promotions.

Nancy's blessing beyond the crown – Restoration…

Betsy Allen

Betsy Allen only competed in my pageant once, and honestly I didn't get to know her all that well, but three months after the pageant I received a letter that touched me in a very profound way. Here is an excerpt from that letter:

I cannot believe that it has been three months since the 2001 pageant! Wow, how time flies. Now that things have settled down, I just want to thank you for directing and coordinating such a wonderful event. I learned a lot about myself from participating this year and remembered why I enjoy pageants so much.

Something else sad and wonderful happened as a result of this event. As we all know, the Lord works in mysterious ways. Long story short, my sister, along with some other family members, came to the pageant to support me. (They all traveled from out of state.) *If you remember, my husband left for military training the day before the pageant. My sister had been to several doctors regarding some health problems she had been experiencing for a few years. My husband, Ron, and my sister spent one day together before Ron left for Texas.* (Her husband was a medical doctor.)

The night before he left, he told me that I had to persuade my sister to go back to the doctor. He thought she might have Acromegaly, which is a rare, life-threatening disease if not treated. It turned out to be a correct diagnosis. She had surgery in July and is now on her way to recovery. If you wonder how I am going to tie this all together, I know that my sister probably would not have visited us until Christmas if I had not participated in this pageant. The longer the disease continues—the reduced chance for a full recovery. In my heart I know that it was meant for me to participate in order to get my sister to visit. It may sound silly, but I am just thankful that things worked out the way they did for her!

Betsy's blessing beyond the crown – Divine Intervention...

Terry Vincent

Terry Vincent was the most beautiful fifty-six-year-old woman I have ever met. Apparently I wasn't the only one to notice; a stranger approached her at the gym where she was working out and suggested that she enter the Mrs. Colorado Pageant.

Not only was she physically beautiful, but a genuinely beautiful spirit as well. She was the very definition of superwoman. She was a wife of many years, mother to four attractive, successful grown children, and worked as a nurse in hospice care. At the age of fifty-six this was her first pageant competition.

She was easy to work with and truly enjoyed every stage of preparation. When the pageant was over she sent me a photo taken at her "post-pageant celebration" with her four children playfully holding her in the position of a Greek goddess. Also enclosed was a copy of a poem that her twenty-year-old son, Christopher, had written and given to her just before the pageant began. It meant the world to her.

My Mother

In no more than a week, you'll go up on stage.
To stand among women of much younger age.

Judges will score you, your beauty, your smile.
They'll look at your stance, and your glamorous style.

How cherished you are, they will not know.
Your family, your friends, for the fruits that you sow.

But I've had the pleasure of seeing inside,
Your kindness of heart, and your passionate side.

So I'll look up at you, as you wave to the crowd.
And I'll smile to myself, as I'll be so proud.

Four of us you've raised, with kindness and love.
To be strong of heart, and look to Him above.

For the stories you read, the meals you cook.
The love that you gave, and the pain that you took.

I thank you, Sweet Mother, for all that you've done.
For giving me life, and calling me son.

This poem is for you, I hope it will touch.
Your beautiful heart that I love so much.

By Christopher Vincent

There's probably a moment in every mother's life when she finally gets the praise that she deserves. I remember one such day, shortly after I was married. I called my mother from a pay phone at a Safeway grocery store; apparently I was so struck with gratitude that I couldn't even wait to get home to make the call. *Now I was in charge of meal planning and I really didn't enjoy it!* I wanted to thank her for all the cooking she had done which seemingly had gone unnoticed for so many years. This was Terry's moment.

Terry's blessing beyond the crown – Recognition...

Niles Mayo

I've always been a hopeless sentimentalist when it comes to patriotism. I've always had a healthy appreciation for my country and the people who keep it a free place on this planet. My father, my hero, was a Marine and is a combat veteran of the Korean War. My productions always started off with the singing of the national anthem and I always had a military color guard to present the flag. I loved it! It never failed to give me goose bumps when they would ceremoniously march on stage to kick off our event.

160

In 2004 the war in Iraq had made it nearly impossible to procure a military color guard for civilian appearances. So I purchased two huge American flags to be flown in on the theater line set and resigned myself to the fact that I wouldn't have the military represented during the singing of the *Star Spangled Banner*.

During the tech rehearsal on Saturday, my husband casually suggested that in lieu of a color guard we feature the military husbands of our contestants instead. It was a brilliant idea! One of the husbands served in the Navy, one was a captain in the Air Force, and one a Vietnam Veteran. As the curtain rose it slowly revealed these three men saluting our country's flag.

Niles Mayo was married to Kelly, Mrs. Denver 2004. At the age of eighteen Niles had enlisted in the Marine Corps during the Vietnam War. When interviewing him for this segment I asked, "Why the Marines?" And he responded, "Because I wanted to be the best."

Seven months into his tour his foot became entangled in a wire designed to set off a landmine. His right leg was blown off and his left leg was severely damaged. Having lost an enormous amount of blood, Niles literally fought for his life in the N.S.A. hospital in the underground bunkers of Danang. It was there, a week later in his hospital bed that a general distinguished him with the Purple Heart and the Bronze Star Combat V (a medal awarded for fighting with valor). Once stabilized, he was flown to Guam for further treatment and was ultimately sent to the VA Medical Center in Philadelphia to recover for nearly a year.

In 2004 Niles was being fitted for a new prosthetic leg and was experiencing uncommon pain and discomfort. My staff made a concerted effort to make sure that he didn't have to stand in line or remain on his feet any longer than necessary. So when we asked him to stand on stage for the singing of the national anthem I wasn't sure it would be physically possible. Much to my delight he agreed and an idea that began as almost an afterthought ended up becoming an exceptional moment in the 2004 pageant production.

A week later we received this letter:

Dear Russell and Tricia,

For many years I have carried the Marine Corps in my heart and soul. I have always been and will forever be a Marine. People have always referred to me as a Vietnam Vet, but I have never felt any pride in that title...until the night of the pageant. That night you made me feel so proud to be called a Veteran.

Enclosed you will find the first Purple Heart I ever received, and I want you to have it.

From one old Marine to, two very special people. Thanks for the Memories!

Niles L. Mayo, Sr.

It was such an incomprehensible gesture. Russell and I stood speechless in the kitchen, where I had opened the mail. I can't recall a time in my career when I had felt so honored and yet so disturbed as to why it had taken a passing moment at a "pageant" to make this man feel appreciated for his personal sacrifice. I framed the Purple Heart and displayed it in my office for one year and then appropriately I returned it to its rightful owner, Mr. Niles Mayo—Proud Marine—Vietnam Veteran—American Hero!

Kelly and Niles' blessing beyond the crown – Appreciation...

Lynne McNichol

Lynne McNichol was a thirty-three-year-old single mother of three suffering from what she believed to be a toothache. After visiting her family dentist he informed her that she more than likely needed a root canal and referred her to an oral surgeon.

For several months Lynne put off scheduling the appointment due to a lack of funds. Finally the pain became too unbearable so she borrowed the money from her father and made time to see the oral surgeon. After the customary x-rays were taken, the doctor requested that she call her family. The news that day was devastating. By 5:00 p.m. she, along with her mother and sister, found themselves in the office of an oncologist. The official diagnosis was adenoid cystic carcinoma. In the honest words of the doctor he informed Lynne that most people don't survive this form of cancer and for those who do, spend the rest of their lives disfigured and in pain. Reeling from the initial shock, Lynne later told me she remembered thinking, "Dying is *not* an option—I'm a single mother and I have three children to raise!"

She had her first surgery to remove the malignant tumor in 1989. Along with the tumor doctors removed the pallet of her mouth, her sinuses, a tear duck, all but five of her teeth and all of her gums on the right side of her face. And then of course she was subjected to extensive chemotherapy. Besides the physical pain, Lynne endured the emotional trauma of her disfigurement and didn't leave the seclusion of her home for many months. She had survived, but her self-confidence and dignity had been shattered.

Since her original surgery, Lynne had eleven subsequent surgeries including several to reconstruct her face. Through the pain and anguish Lynne remained hopeful and optimistic. In 1994 she married her second husband, John McNichol and had two more children—both boys.

Adenoid cystic carcinoma is considered one of the deadliest cancers and a survivor is not considered fully cured until they are cancer free for twenty years. In 2007 Lynne was counting down to year twenty and decided to enter the Mrs. Colorado Pageant. No longer paralyzed by her disfigurement she represented the city of Limon in the annual competition to reclaim the self-confidence she had lost so many years ago.

That year an essay contest determined the annual winner of the "Crowning Achievement" award judged by Marney Duckworth, the founder of the Mrs. Colorado Foundation. Lynne's story was deemed the winning essay and along with the award, the foundation also provided her with a complete home computer system. It was a proud moment for Lynne and when asked to give the audience a brief synopsis of her essay she eloquently relayed her story with charm and humility. It was hard to imagine that winning was such a surprise given the magnitude of her personal story of tragedy and triumph.

Later I asked her, "What would you like to share with the women of Colorado?" She said with heartfelt conviction:

"I'd just encourage people to never give up, and if you have a dream like entering a pageant, you shouldn't be afraid to go for it!"
~ Lynne McNichol – Mrs. Limon 2007

Lynne's blessing beyond the crown – Celebration…

Melissa Kraft

On June 21, 2002, I was diagnosed with a large tumor located in the center of my brain. Because of its size and the fact that I was now going blind I had very little time to research a surgeon and have it removed. As scary as it was, the diagnosis was actually a blessing, as I had been sick for many years with painful headaches and other debilitating symptoms. The tumor was successfully removed making July 3 my personal Independence Day. Thank God my vision was fully restored and I was now on the pathway to recovery. It's just that recovery was a much longer road than I had anticipated and one of the most heartbreaking side effects was the loss of my hair. It was now just dried up stubble and there were visible bald spots appearing on the top of my scalp.

If it sounds like vanity, you're right! There were days when I experienced profound joy because I was alive and then there were those days when

I suffered such embarrassment and an unexplainable diminished self-esteem with the loss of my hair. And the irony of it all was that I was working in an image-based industry. It was truly hard to reconcile my feelings, but I wasn't ready to abandon my career because I somehow didn't look good enough to fit the role.

The upshot is that as a result of my personal experience I've developed a keen sense of compassion for people who lose a piece of their identity when illness robs them of a physical ability or trait.

Sometime around Christmas my husband had given me a gift certificate to a nearby day spa for a pedicure/manicure. I looked forward to the luxury, but once I sat down under the glare of the nail technician's lamp I became extremely uncomfortable. I fidgeted in my seat trying to position myself so that the light wouldn't fall upon the top of my head. I felt myself becoming agitated and I began to complain about a simple mix-up in the order of the services.

I finally apologized for my actions and explained that I had recently undergone surgery to remove a brain tumor and was embarrassed of my hair loss. Honesty *is* liberating. The nail tech looked up from my hands and exclaimed, "My mother-in-law had a brain tumor and is now battling brain cancer." I felt ashamed that I was fussing over thinning hair when this woman was facing the loss of her life—I asked for her name. I like to specifically pray for people by name—it was Romaine.

Becca became my regular "nail girl" and I followed her from salon to salon. I saw her on an average of once a month and asked for regular updates on her mother-in-law's condition. Because of my own experience with a brain tumor and the devastating after effects, I honestly never missed a night to whisper a brief prayer on behalf of Romaine, who I had never met. About a year later Becca informed me that Romaine had lost her battle with cancer. For a while, I can't remember how long, I continued to pray for her family—that God would grant them the "peace that passeth all understanding."

In 2007 I was conducting business as usual. I had now designated just one day a week to consult with contestants and on this particular day I had already seen three contestants back to back when in walked, Melissa Kraft. We introduced ourselves and as I welcomed her into my office I had the overwhelming sense that I knew her, so I asked if we had ever met. She looked me in the eyes and casually answered, "No."

I then asked her if perhaps I looked familiar and she briefly studied my face and again casually answered, "No." There was just something about her countenance, I couldn't let it go so I inquired about her employment, had she ever worked at a nearby grocery store, post office or department store; somewhere very public where our paths might have crossed, and again she answered, this time with great assurance, "No." So we both sat down and I began my "introduction to pageantry" spiel.

Sometime nearing the end of the consultation I asked her how she had heard about the pageant and she told me that her sister-in-law, Becca, had encouraged her to enter.

Ah! Becca, my nail girl! But I still hadn't made the connection. Before leaving my office I always put the contestants through a four minute mock interview so they know what to expect at the time of competition. It also gave me a sense of their communication skills under fire. I began by asking her some fairly routine questions based on her initial application and then I asked one of my favorite questions. It really helps me gauge how open and real a contestant is willing to be. I asked her "What is the hardest thing you have ever done?" I really don't remember her initial answer because she was searching for something to say and the end result was not at all compelling.

And then it dawned on me! There in my office sat the beautiful daughter of Romaine Blake; the woman who I had prayed for every night for over a year. So now that I had some insight into her life, unbeknownst to her, I reworded the question and asked, "If you could change one thing about your life, what would you change and why?"

She looked at me, tears welled up in her eyes and she said, "My mother died."

I interrupted her and said, "She died of a brain tumor didn't she?"

Melissa nodded her head in disbelief.

I continued, "And her name was Romaine." Okay, now Melissa is looking at me like I'm a mystic.

I went on, "I never met your mother, but I prayed for her every night for over a year and now here sits her beautiful daughter in my office." By now we were both choking back tears.

She went on to explain, "If I could change one thing it would be that I never told my mom that I loved her."

Again I stopped her in astonishment, "You mean to tell me that you knew your mother was dying and you never told her that you loved her?"

She continued with her explanation, "I felt like if I said the words, I was accepting the fact that she was going to die and I just didn't want to do that to her."

For a moment, things got foggy and I reflected back to the day that I received the call confirming my own diagnosis. I had immediately called my husband on his cell phone and told him that it was true. I really did have a brain tumor. He responded as if I had just given him the weather report. In a somewhat sing-song voice he said something like, "Really? Oh, hmm, well now we know." And that pretty much ended the conversation. Several years later, at a dinner party, I overheard him recounting that day to a friend. He told him that when he got my phone call he pulled over to the side of the road and cried.

"Wait a minute," I interjected, "You cried? Why didn't you let me know how you *really* felt?"

Russell looked me in the eyes and said with a steely sound to his voice, "You didn't need for me to fall apart; you needed me to be intact. You needed me to take care of things, so I wasn't about to let you know how afraid I was."

I shared my experience with Melissa and assured her that she had made the right decision. It was truly a gift for her mother to leave this world knowing that her daughter would be all right.

It's funny how people are woven into our lives—or maybe not. Is it coincidence? Maybe nothing is truly a coincidence. For whatever reason, I felt that our chance association was a Divine encounter. She was able to confirm my experience and hopefully I was able to confirm hers. It was a unique and indescribable moment that I personally consider to have been a real blessing.

Melissa's blessing beyond the crown – Validation...

Evie Loomis

I met Evelynn Loomis during the first four months as the Colorado state director in 1992. She was an effervescent, thirty-year-old flight attendant with three small children. She didn't have a big budget to compete, so she purchased her gown that year from a consignment shop. It was a gold, fully beaded dress adorned with strands of beads that dangled. It was a bit outdated, but beautiful in its own right. That year she placed sixth out of fourteen contestants.

Evie embodies the meaning of perseverance and returned in 1993 to place second runner-up. She would ultimately compete for eleven of my seventeen years as the director. I couldn't help but become friends with her over the years and we kept in touch even when she didn't compete. I can truly say that if I could have wished it so, I would have given anything to have seen her be crowned Mrs. Colorado. I can't imagine a more deserving person, but in fact it just wasn't meant to be.

After a long hiatus she returned to pageant competition in the spring of 2006. That year during our final tech rehearsal I decided that she would be our "rehearsal winner." We called fourth runner-up, then third runner-up, then second runner-up and finally after the standard little spiel about should the winner not be able to perform her duties the first runner-up will assume the crown and all the benefits of the title, we announced the first runner-up, and the rehearsal winner is—drum roll—contestant number forty-four, Evie Loomis! The crowning music played, she was presented with the banner, the crown put atop her head, the bouquet of roses placed in her arms and when she turned to walk the winning walk, tears streamed down her face taking everyone by surprise. After all this was *just* a rehearsal.

By then the other contestants were tearing up as well. I didn't *dare* go there because I had to co-emcee the event that evening and couldn't afford a break in my stride. But I stood back and reveled in her emotions. She was finally getting the moment that she had only dreamed about! What a lady, what a friend, what a true inspiration. That year the fifty contestants overwhelmingly voted to award her with the Mrs. Congeniality title and deservedly so. She personified the very essence of a winner!

In January of 2008 after much prayer and deliberation I decided that I would retire as the Colorado state director once the 2008 production was over. While I knew it was the right decision for me I was conflicted about it nonetheless. I called Evie up and asked her to compete one more time. I told her, "You were there when I started and it only seems right that we go out together!" With little time to prepare she happily agreed with no hesitation. At that point only a handful of people were informed of my decision and for professional reasons it had to stay that way.

The 2008 pageant weekend was bittersweet, but I was sharing every minute with my friend, Evie. During our top five finale where everyone receives a "Finisher's Medal" and only the top five continue to compete I looked up from the podium as Evie made her way down from center stage to receive her medal. I drew a quick breath and my eyes filled with tears as she walked toward me and rounded the corner of the stage no longer wearing the new, red evening gown she had purchased to compete in, but rather her gold, beaded gown with ornamental, dangling embellishments. As she passed the podium she just gave me a wink. She had worn the very first gown she'd ever competed in as a tribute to our friendship and to this strange journey of competition we call pageantry.

Evie's blessing beyond the crown – Connection...

While writing this manuscript I was invited to attend my good friend, Brian Kelly's retirement party. It was a celebration of his thirty years of service as an attorney for the city of Berkeley. Other than a couple of mutual friends, I knew nobody else there and as I expected most of the guests were lawyers or scholars from U.C. Berkeley.

The party was fun, the people were friendly, and many of them went out of their way to make me feel welcome. In passing conversation (more like polite small talk), a male acquaintance asked me what I was doing now that I had retired. I told him I was writing a book.

He looked at me with a sarcastic grin, then raised both his hands to resemble that of a large cat and made a hissing sound. "You mean that kind of a book?" He was annoying, for sure, but it really was kind of funny.

Of course I smiled and with an inaudible sigh politely said, "No it's not that kind of a book."

He persisted, "But surely you must have stories like that?"

I nodded my head in acknowledgment and told him that in seventeen years I could recall a handful of "stories-like-that" but in fact they weren't very noteworthy. I explained that my pageant memoirs were written about the inspiration I had experienced and the exceptional people I had met along the way.

I stood there mindlessly swirling my glass of Merlot and thought, *how sad that because of some lingering, archaic stereotype about women and competition, people really have no clue about pageantry and the women who compete in pageants. They actually believe that the behavior of the participants resemble that of cast members on a bad reality show rather than an All-American sport.*

He kept talking, but my eyes glazed over and I temporarily checked out of the conversation. For whatever reason, I was reliving a memory about a woman named, Barb Valente. I wasn't really sure what year it was, but I was standing outside the room where personal interviews were taking place with the next couple of contestants in line including Barb, when another contestant flew down the hallway in a panic.

She was completely dressed with the exception of her shoes because she had failed to pack them! She looked at me for help, like I would somehow magically be able to produce a pair of shoes that not only matched her suit, but ones that would fit as well. My mind raced for possible solutions when Barb calmly asked her what size she wore.

Right then in the hallway just minutes before her own competition experience was about to begin Barb slipped her shoes off and lent them to her competitor.

For a moment I considered sharing this little vignette with him as a way to defend the pageant industry or moreover to defend the character of women in competition. But ultimately I decided to abandon the conversation altogether—there was no need to defend my career path—there was no need to defend pageantry—and there was no need to defend the remarkable women whom I adored.

The reality is that I loved every minute of my seventeen years as the director to the Mrs. Colorado Pageant. I would do it all over again. In fact, my only regret is that I wish I would have had the stamina to continue. I feel enriched to have had the opportunity to work with the women who participated, and that the relationships I developed over the years had filled a vacuum in my life.

In some strange way it felt like my destiny. I believe that everyone is blessed with gifts and I think mine was to cheer others to success.

People ask me, "What's next?" I have some ideas, but nothing in concrete. I think I'll just sit back and listen to the rhythm of life and see where it takes me...

Blessings Beyond The Crown

The Take Away

- View every competition as an opportunity to grow in character and spirit.
- Before competing ask yourself—besides winning what else would I like to gain from this experience?
- After competing—win—lose—or draw be mindful of looking for the "not so obvious" benefit from the experience.
- Remember that sometimes the reward isn't the trophy, medal or crown at the end of the day; it's the experience that will shape you for future opportunities.

Raeanne Smith – Mrs. Colorado 2000

Acknowledgments

"At times our own light goes out and is rekindled by a spark from another person. Each of us has cause to think with deep gratitude of those who have lighted the flame within us."
~ Albert Schweitzer – Theologian and Philosopher

First and foremost I want to honor my God and Savior, Jesus Christ—with Him all things *are* possible.

To my husband, Russell, who once paid me the highest compliment a husband could give a wife, *"Life with you has never been boring."* Russell you have been the partner of a lifetime.

I want to thank my parents, Hayden and Patricia Woods, for always modeling perseverance and determination with grace, even when life dealt them *serious* challenges. You *are* my heroes.

To my family, Julia, Ara, Joshua, "Brother Bill," Aunt Hannah and Uncle Harlan—thanks for all the help. The productions truly were a family affair.

To my editor, Karen Reddick, The Red Pen Editor; thanks for keeping me on point with your grammar skills, encouragement and honesty.

To Nick Zelinger of NZ Graphics, quite possibly the most patient man on the planet, thanks for coupling vision with creativity to produce the design for this book.

To the Mrs. Colorado titleholders, Sharon Nuanes, 1981; Toni Neibauer, 1982; Colleen Adolfson, 1985; Laurie Kole-Wallace, 1986; Toni Ford-Cole, 1990; Blair Wellman-Morgan, 1991; Janet Horvath, 1992; Debbie Barnhill, 1993; Debi Moore, 1994; Paula Aurand-Stephens, 1995; Amy Nugent, 1996; Diandre Warren, 1997; Gina

DelVecchio, 1998; Shae Stuard, 1999; Raeanne Smith-Duca, 2000; Traci Holman-Todd, 2001; Emily Stark, 2002; Elisabeth Cartmill, 2003; Sheri Engstrom, 2004; Jennifer Lamont, 2005; Marney Duckworth, 2006; Tiffany Sawyer, 2007; Christina Sacha, 2008; Megan Yarberry, 2009 and Shalon Polson, 2010; each of you have taught me valuable lessons during the ups and downs of my career and many of you have become my dearest friends.

To the Mrs. Colorado contestants; each year hundreds of women called me to inquire about entering the pageant and countless others sat in the audience year after year and only dreamed of entering, but *you* were the courageous cast of characters that made this program soar!

To the friends I made along the way, Lizabeth Morrow-Nold, Carol & Lee Beckler, Doug Werner, Virginia Stephens, Anne Davies, Lynne Arne, Jerry Wittkoff, Nick Carter, Steve Crecelius, Carol Winberg, Kelly Loggins, Lisa Henry, Muriel Blacksher-Martinez, Rita Case, Danielle Grosse, LaDonna Griego, Mike & Loni Kallay, Joe & Marcie Aceto, Joanne Holzer, Barb Fischer, Dennis Roberts, Jennifer Bradley, Jim Ratts, Ed Rothschild, Michael Rassmusen, Kirk Lambert, D.J. Mc Dermott, Kristianna Nichols, Lisa Holtz-O'Dell, Muchion Hughes, Michael Bondi, Megan Anderson, Kari Kisch, Albert Sainz, Dave Wilson, Jeannette Murrietta, Kevin Hutchin, Randy Holman, Joetta Schumann, Rosie Herndon; you've made my world a more colorful place.

To David and Elaine Marmel the "couple" behind the Mrs. America name; thank you for giving me the opportunity to serve as the Colorado State Director. I believe in destiny and becoming a part of your organization over twenty-one years ago changed the course of my life. I'm impoverished for words of gratitude.

And to two men whom I've only met while standing in line to buy an autographed book, Dr. Robert H. Schuller and Mr. Dennis Prager; you have influenced the way I view my faith and look at my world. Please continue to be a beacon of light to all those who listen to your positive words of vision and hope.

Diandre Warren – Mrs. Colorado 1997

About the Author

Tricia has been involved in the field of pageantry for over twenty-three years as a contestant, titleholder, director/producer, consultant, emcee and judge. In 1985, she danced with the Pure Gold, cheerleaders for the Denver Gold USFL football team, and in 1987 appeared as a finalist on the popular variety/competition show, *Puttin' on the Hits.*

She has worked for several Colorado talent agencies as a print model and in 1989 captured the Mrs. Colorado crown on her third try. She's a two time "Best in Evening Gown" award winner and the recipient of a national "Most Photogenic" award. She became Colorado's Executive State Director to the Mrs. America Pageant system in 1992, and in 1995 was honored to receive the national Seymour Sietz Award for "Director of the Year."

In 2009 Tricia was a national finalist in the American Heart Association's annual search for the Go Red for Women spokesperson. And in 2010 she and her mother, Patricia, were selected to serve as ambassadors for Colorado's 2010 Go Red for Women Survivor Gallery.

She's also a big supporter of the Denver Rescue Mission, as well as Veteran's Hospital, and was recognized by Governor Bill Owens with an "Honorary Proclamation" proclaiming June 13, 2001 as Mrs. Colorado Day for her commitment to the community. She's been married to her husband, Russell, for thirty-three years and is currently working as a motivational presenter for Girl Speak Enterprises.

Shae Stuard – Mrs. Colorado 1999

"God doesn't require us to succeed; he only requires that you try."

~ Mother Teresa